Herman Melville: A Very Short Introduction

VERY SHORT INTRODUCTIONS are for anyone wanting a stimulating and accessible way into a new subject. They are written by experts, and have been translated into more than 45 different languages.

The series began in 1995, and now covers a wide variety of topics in every discipline. The VSI library currently contains over 750 volumes—a Very Short Introduction to everything from Psychology and Philosophy of Science to American History and Relativity—and continues to grow in every subject area.

Very Short Introductions available now:

ABOLITIONISM Richard S. Newman
THE ABRAHAMIC RELIGIONS
  Charles L. Cohen
ACCOUNTING Christopher Nobes
ADDICTION Keith Humphreys
ADOLESCENCE Peter K. Smith
THEODOR W. ADORNO
  Andrew Bowie
ADVERTISING Winston Fletcher
AERIAL WARFARE Frank Ledwidge
AESTHETICS Bence Nanay
AFRICAN AMERICAN HISTORY
  Jonathan Scott Holloway
AFRICAN AMERICAN RELIGION
  Eddie S. Glaude Jr.
AFRICAN HISTORY John Parker and
  Richard Rathbone
AFRICAN POLITICS Ian Taylor
AFRICAN RELIGIONS
  Jacob K. Olupona
AGATHA CHRISTIE Gill Plain
AGEING Nancy A. Pachana
AGNOSTICISM Robin Le Poidevin
AGRICULTURE Paul Brassley and
  Richard Soffe
ALEXANDER THE GREAT
  Hugh Bowden
ALGEBRA Peter M. Higgins
AMERICAN BUSINESS HISTORY
  Walter A. Friedman
AMERICAN CULTURAL HISTORY
  Eric Avila
AMERICAN FOREIGN RELATIONS
  Andrew Preston
AMERICAN HISTORY Paul S. Boyer
AMERICAN IMMIGRATION
  David A. Gerber
AMERICAN INTELLECTUAL
  HISTORY
  Jennifer Ratner-Rosenhagen
THE AMERICAN JUDICIAL SYSTEM
  Charles L. Zelden
AMERICAN LEGAL HISTORY
  G. Edward White
AMERICAN MILITARY HISTORY
  Joseph T. Glatthaar
AMERICAN NAVAL HISTORY
  Craig L. Symonds
AMERICAN POETRY David Caplan
AMERICAN POLITICAL HISTORY
  Donald Critchlow
AMERICAN POLITICAL PARTIES
  AND ELECTIONS L. Sandy Maisel
AMERICAN POLITICS
  Richard M. Valelly
THE AMERICAN PRESIDENCY
  Charles O. Jones
THE AMERICAN REVOLUTION
  Robert J. Allison
AMERICAN SLAVERY
  Heather Andrea Williams
THE AMERICAN SOUTH
  Charles Reagan Wilson
THE AMERICAN WEST Stephen Aron
AMERICAN WOMEN'S
  HISTORY Susan Ware
AMPHIBIANS T. S. Kemp
ANAESTHESIA Aidan O'Donnell

ANALYTIC PHILOSOPHY
    Michael Beaney
ANARCHISM Alex Prichard
ANCIENT ASSYRIA Karen Radner
ANCIENT EGYPT Ian Shaw
ANCIENT EGYPTIAN ART AND
    ARCHITECTURE Christina Riggs
ANCIENT GREECE Paul Cartledge
ANCIENT GREEK AND
    ROMAN SCIENCE Liba Taub
THE ANCIENT NEAR EAST
    Amanda H. Podany
ANCIENT PHILOSOPHY Julia Annas
ANCIENT WARFARE
    Harry Sidebottom
ANGELS David Albert Jones
ANGLICANISM Mark Chapman
THE ANGLO-SAXON AGE John Blair
ANIMAL BEHAVIOUR
    Tristram D. Wyatt
THE ANIMAL KINGDOM
    Peter Holland
ANIMAL RIGHTS David DeGrazia
ANSELM Thomas Williams
THE ANTARCTIC Klaus Dodds
ANTHROPOCENE Erle C. Ellis
ANTISEMITISM Steven Beller
ANXIETY Daniel Freeman and
    Jason Freeman
THE APOCRYPHAL GOSPELS
    Paul Foster
APPLIED MATHEMATICS
    Alain Goriely
THOMAS AQUINAS Fergus Kerr
ARBITRATION Thomas Schultz and
    Thomas Grant
ARCHAEOLOGY Paul Bahn
ARCHITECTURE Andrew Ballantyne
THE ARCTIC Klaus Dodds and
    Jamie Woodward
HANNAH ARENDT Dana Villa
ARISTOCRACY William Doyle
ARISTOTLE Jonathan Barnes
ART HISTORY Dana Arnold
ART THEORY Cynthia Freeland
ARTIFICIAL INTELLIGENCE
    Margaret A. Boden
ASIAN AMERICAN HISTORY
    Madeline Y. Hsu
ASTROBIOLOGY David C. Catling
ASTROPHYSICS James Binney
ATHEISM Julian Baggini
THE ATMOSPHERE Paul I. Palmer
AUGUSTINE Henry Chadwick
JANE AUSTEN Tom Keymer
AUSTRALIA Kenneth Morgan
AUTHORITARIANISM James Loxton
AUTISM Uta Frith
AUTOBIOGRAPHY Laura Marcus
THE AVANT GARDE David Cottington
THE AZTECS David Carrasco
BABYLONIA Trevor Bryce
BACTERIA Sebastian G. B. Amyes
BANKING John Goddard and
    John O. S. Wilson
BARTHES Jonathan Culler
THE BEATS David Sterritt
BEAUTY Roger Scruton
LUDWIG VAN BEETHOVEN
    Mark Evan Bonds
BEHAVIOURAL ECONOMICS
    Michelle Baddeley
BESTSELLERS John Sutherland
THE BIBLE John Riches
BIBLICAL ARCHAEOLOGY
    Eric H. Cline
BIG DATA Dawn E. Holmes
BIOCHEMISTRY Mark Lorch
BIODIVERSITY CONSERVATION
    David Macdonald
BIOGEOGRAPHY Mark V. Lomolino
BIOGRAPHY Hermione Lee
BIOMETRICS Michael Fairhurst
ELIZABETH BISHOP
    Jonathan F. S. Post
BLACK HOLES Katherine Blundell
BLASPHEMY Yvonne Sherwood
BLOOD Chris Cooper
THE BLUES Elijah Wald
THE BODY Chris Shilling
THE BOHEMIANS David Weir
NIELS BOHR J. L. Heilbron
THE BOOK OF COMMON PRAYER
    Brian Cummings
THE BOOK OF MORMON
    Terryl Givens
BORDERS Alexander C. Diener and
    Joshua Hagen
JORGE LUIS BORGES Ilan Stavans
THE BRAIN Michael O'Shea

BRANDING Robert Jones
THE BRICS Andrew F. Cooper
BRITISH ARCHITECTURE
    Dana Arnold
BRITISH CINEMA Charles Barr
THE BRITISH CONSTITUTION
    Martin Loughlin
THE BRITISH EMPIRE Ashley Jackson
BRITISH POLITICS Tony Wright
BUDDHA Michael Carrithers
BUDDHISM Damien Keown
BUDDHIST ETHICS Damien Keown
BYZANTIUM Peter Sarris
CALVINISM Jon Balserak
ALBERT CAMUS Oliver Gloag
CANADA Donald Wright
CANCER Nicholas James
CAPITALISM James Fulcher
CATHOLICISM Gerald O'Collins
THE CATHOLIC REFORMATION
    James E. Kelly
CAUSATION Stephen Mumford and
    Rani Lill Anjum
THE CELL Terence Allen and
    Graham Cowling
THE CELTS Barry Cunliffe
CHAOS Leonard Smith
GEOFFREY CHAUCER David Wallace
CHEMISTRY Peter Atkins
CHILD PSYCHOLOGY Usha Goswami
CHILDREN'S LITERATURE
    Kimberley Reynolds
CHINESE LITERATURE Sabina Knight
CHOICE THEORY Michael Allingham
CHRISTIAN ART Beth Williamson
CHRISTIAN ETHICS D. Stephen Long
CHRISTIANITY Linda Woodhead
CICERO Yelena Baraz
CIRCADIAN RHYTHMS
    Russell Foster and Leon Kreitzman
CITIZENSHIP Richard Bellamy
CITY PLANNING Carl Abbott
CIVIL ENGINEERING
    David Muir Wood
THE CIVIL RIGHTS MOVEMENT
    Thomas C. Holt
CIVIL WARS Monica Duffy Toft
CLASSICAL LITERATURE William Allan
CLASSICAL MYTHOLOGY
    Helen Morales
CLASSICS Mary Beard and
    John Henderson
CLAUSEWITZ Michael Howard
CLIMATE Mark Maslin
CLIMATE CHANGE Mark Maslin
CLINICAL PSYCHOLOGY
    Susan Llewelyn and
    Katie Aafjes-van Doorn
COGNITIVE BEHAVIOURAL
    THERAPY Freda McManus
COGNITIVE NEUROSCIENCE
    Richard Passingham
THE COLD WAR Robert J. McMahon
COLONIAL AMERICA Alan Taylor
COLONIAL LATIN AMERICAN
    LITERATURE Rolena Adorno
COMBINATORICS Robin Wilson
COMEDY Matthew Bevis
COMMUNISM Leslie Holmes
COMPARATIVE LAW Sabrina Ragone
    and Guido Smorto
COMPARATIVE LITERATURE
    Ben Hutchinson
COMPETITION AND
    ANTITRUST LAW Ariel Ezrachi
COMPLEXITY John H. Holland
THE COMPUTER Darrel Ince
COMPUTER SCIENCE
    Subrata Dasgupta
CONCENTRATION CAMPS
    Dan Stone
CONDENSED MATTER PHYSICS
    Ross H. McKenzie
CONFUCIANISM Daniel K. Gardner
THE CONQUISTADORS
    Matthew Restall and
    Felipe Fernández-Armesto
CONSCIENCE Paul Strohm
CONSCIOUSNESS Susan Blackmore
CONTEMPORARY ART
    Julian Stallabrass
CONTEMPORARY FICTION
    Robert Eaglestone
CONTINENTAL PHILOSOPHY
    Simon Critchley
COPERNICUS Owen Gingerich
CORAL REEFS Charles Sheppard
CORPORATE SOCIAL
    RESPONSIBILITY Jeremy Moon
CORRUPTION Leslie Holmes

COSMOLOGY Peter Coles
COUNTRY MUSIC Richard Carlin
CREATIVITY Vlad Glăveanu
CRIME FICTION Richard Bradford
CRIMINAL JUSTICE Julian V. Roberts
CRIMINOLOGY Tim Newburn
CRITICAL THEORY
    Stephen Eric Bronner
THE CRUSADES Christopher Tyerman
CRYPTOGRAPHY Sean Murphy and
    Rachel Player
CRYSTALLOGRAPHY A. M. Glazer
THE CULTURAL REVOLUTION
    Richard Curt Kraus
DADA AND SURREALISM
    David Hopkins
DANTE Peter Hainsworth and
    David Robey
DARWIN Jonathan Howard
THE DEAD SEA SCROLLS
    Timothy H. Lim
DECADENCE David Weir
DECOLONIZATION Dane Kennedy
DEMENTIA Kathleen Taylor
DEMOCRACY Naomi Zack
DEMOGRAPHY Sarah Harper
DEPRESSION Jan Scott and
    Mary Jane Tacchi
DERRIDA Simon Glendinning
DESCARTES Tom Sorell
DESERTS Nick Middleton
DESIGN John Heskett
DEVELOPMENT Ian Goldin
DEVELOPMENTAL BIOLOGY
    Lewis Wolpert
THE DEVIL Darren Oldridge
DIASPORA Kevin Kenny
CHARLES DICKENS Jenny Hartley
DICTIONARIES Lynda Mugglestone
DINOSAURS David Norman
DIPLOMATIC HISTORY
    Joseph M. Siracusa
DOCUMENTARY FILM
    Patricia Aufderheide
DOSTOEVSKY Deborah Martinsen
DREAMING J. Allan Hobson
DRUGS Les Iversen
DRUIDS Barry Cunliffe
DYNASTY Jeroen Duindam
DYSLEXIA Margaret J. Snowling

EARLY MUSIC Thomas Forrest Kelly
THE EARTH Martin Redfern
EARTH SYSTEM SCIENCE Tim Lenton
ECOLOGY Jaboury Ghazoul
ECONOMICS Partha Dasgupta
EDUCATION Gary Thomas
EGYPTIAN MYTH Geraldine Pinch
EIGHTEENTH-CENTURY BRITAIN
    Paul Langford
ELECTIONS L. Sandy Maisel and
    Jennifer A. Yoder
THE ELEMENTS Philip Ball
GEORGE ELIOT Juliette Atkinson
EMOTION Dylan Evans
EMPIRE Stephen Howe
EMPLOYMENT LAW David Cabrelli
ENERGY SYSTEMS Nick Jenkins
ENGELS Terrell Carver
ENGINEERING David Blockley
THE ENGLISH LANGUAGE
    Simon Horobin
ENGLISH LITERATURE Jonathan Bate
THE ENLIGHTENMENT
    John Robertson
ENTREPRENEURSHIP Paul Westhead
    and Mike Wright
ENTROPY James Binney
ENVIRONMENTAL
    ECONOMICS Stephen Smith
ENVIRONMENTAL ETHICS
    Robin Attfield
ENVIRONMENTAL LAW
    Elizabeth Fisher
ENVIRONMENTAL POLITICS
    Andrew Dobson
ENZYMES Paul Engel
THE EPIC Anthony Welch
EPICUREANISM Catherine Wilson
EPIDEMIOLOGY Rodolfo Saracci
ETHICS Simon Blackburn
ETHNOMUSICOLOGY Timothy Rice
THE ETRUSCANS Christopher Smith
EUGENICS Philippa Levine
THE EUROPEAN UNION
    Simon Usherwood and John Pinder
EUROPEAN UNION LAW
    Anthony Arnull
EVANGELICALISM
    John G. Stackhouse Jr.
EVIL Luke Russell

EVOLUTION Brian and
    Deborah Charlesworth
EXISTENTIALISM Thomas Flynn
EXPLORATION Stewart A. Weaver
EXTINCTION Paul B. Wignall
THE EYE Michael Land
FAIRY TALE Marina Warner
FAITH Roger Trigg
FAMILY LAW Jonathan Herring
MICHAEL FARADAY
    Frank A. J. L. James
FASCISM Kevin Passmore
FASHION Rebecca Arnold
FEDERALISM Mark J. Rozell and
    Clyde Wilcox
FEMINISM Margaret Walters
FEMINIST PHILOSOPHY
    Katharine Jenkins
FILM Michael Wood
FILM MUSIC Kathryn Kalinak
FILM NOIR James Naremore
FIRE Andrew C. Scott
THE FIRST WORLD WAR
    Michael Howard
FLUID MECHANICS Eric Lauga
FOLK MUSIC Mark Slobin
FOOD John Krebs
FORENSIC PSYCHOLOGY
    David Canter
FORENSIC SCIENCE Jim Fraser
FORESTS Jaboury Ghazoul
FOSSILS Keith Thomson
FOUCAULT Gary Gutting
THE FOUNDING FATHERS
    R. B. Bernstein
FRACTALS Kenneth Falconer
FREE SPEECH Nigel Warburton
FREE WILL Thomas Pink
FREEMASONRY Andreas Önnerfors
FRENCH CINEMA Dudley Andrew
FRENCH LITERATURE John D. Lyons
FRENCH PHILOSOPHY
    Stephen Gaukroger and Knox Peden
THE FRENCH REVOLUTION
    William Doyle
FREUD Anthony Storr
FUNDAMENTALISM Malise Ruthven
FUNGI Nicholas P. Money
THE FUTURE Jennifer M. Gidley
FUTURISM Ara Merjian

GALAXIES John Gribbin
GALILEO Stillman Drake
GAME THEORY Ken Binmore
GANDHI Bhikhu Parekh
GARDEN HISTORY Gordon Campbell
GENDER HISTORY Antoinette Burton
GENES Jonathan Slack
GENIUS Andrew Robinson
GENOMICS John Archibald
GEOGRAPHY John Matthews and
    David Herbert
GEOLOGY Jan Zalasiewicz
GEOMETRY Maciej Dunajski
GEOPHYSICAL AND CLIMATE
    HAZARDS Bill McGuire
GEOPHYSICS William Lowrie
GEOPOLITICS Klaus Dodds
GERMAN LITERATURE Nicholas Boyle
GERMAN PHILOSOPHY
    Andrew Bowie
THE GHETTO Bryan Cheyette
GLACIATION David J. A. Evans
GLOBAL ECONOMIC HISTORY
    Robert C. Allen
GLOBAL ISLAM Nile Green
GLOBALIZATION Manfred B. Steger
GOD John Bowker
GÖDEL'S THEOREM A. W. Moore
GOETHE Ritchie Robertson
THE GOTHIC Nick Groom
GOVERNANCE Mark Bevir
GRAVITY Timothy Clifton
THE GREAT DEPRESSION AND
    THE NEW DEAL Eric Rauchway
THE GULAG Alan Barenberg
HABEAS CORPUS Amanda L. Tyler
HABERMAS James Gordon Finlayson
THE HABSBURG EMPIRE
    Martyn Rady
HAPPINESS Daniel M. Haybron
THE HARLEM RENAISSANCE
    Cheryl A. Wall
THE HEBREW BIBLE AS LITERATURE
    Tod Linafelt
HEGEL Peter Singer
HEIDEGGER Michael Inwood
THE HELLENISTIC AGE
    Peter Thonemann
HEREDITY John Waller
HERMENEUTICS Jens Zimmermann

HERODOTUS Jennifer T. Roberts
HIEROGLYPHS Penelope Wilson
HINDUISM Kim Knott
HISTORY John H. Arnold
THE HISTORY OF ASTRONOMY
    Michael Hoskin
THE HISTORY OF CHEMISTRY
    William H. Brock
THE HISTORY OF CHILDHOOD
    James Marten
THE HISTORY OF CINEMA
    Geoffrey Nowell-Smith
THE HISTORY OF COMPUTING
    Doron Swade
THE HISTORY OF EMOTIONS
    Thomas Dixon
THE HISTORY OF LIFE
    Michael Benton
THE HISTORY OF MATHEMATICS
    Jacqueline Stedall
THE HISTORY OF MEDICINE
    William Bynum
THE HISTORY OF PHYSICS
    J. L. Heilbron
THE HISTORY OF POLITICAL
    THOUGHT Richard Whatmore
THE HISTORY OF TIME
    Leofranc Holford-Strevens
HIV AND AIDS Alan Whiteside
HOBBES Richard Tuck
HOLLYWOOD Peter Decherney
THE HOLY ROMAN EMPIRE
    Joachim Whaley
HOME Michael Allen Fox
HOMER Barbara Graziosi
HORACE Llewelyn Morgan
HORMONES Martin Luck
HORROR Darryl Jones
HUMAN ANATOMY
    Leslie Klenerman
HUMAN EVOLUTION Bernard Wood
HUMAN GEOGRAPHY
    Patricia Daley and Ian Klinke
HUMAN PHYSIOLOGY
    Jamie A. Davies
HUMAN RESOURCE
    MANAGEMENT Adrian Wilkinson
HUMAN RIGHTS Andrew Clapham
HUMANISM Stephen Law
HUME James A. Harris
HUMOUR Noël Carroll
IBN SĪNĀ (AVICENNA)
    Peter Adamson
THE ICE AGE Jamie Woodward
IDENTITY Florian Coulmas
IDEOLOGY Michael Freeden
IMAGINATION
    Jennifer Gosetti-Ferencei
THE IMMUNE SYSTEM
    Paul Klenerman
INDIAN CINEMA
    Ashish Rajadhyaksha
INDIAN PHILOSOPHY Sue Hamilton
THE INDUSTRIAL REVOLUTION
    Robert C. Allen
INFECTIOUS DISEASE Marta L. Wayne
    and Benjamin M. Bolker
INFINITY Ian Stewart
INFORMATION Luciano Floridi
INNOVATION Mark Dodgson and
    David Gann
INTELLECTUAL PROPERTY
    Siva Vaidhyanathan
INTELLIGENCE Ian J. Deary
INTERNATIONAL LAW
    Vaughan Lowe
INTERNATIONAL MIGRATION
    Khalid Koser
INTERNATIONAL RELATIONS
    Christian Reus-Smit
INTERNATIONAL SECURITY
    Christopher S. Browning
INSECTS Simon Leather
INVASIVE SPECIES Julie Lockwood and
    Dustin Welbourne
IRAN Ali M. Ansari
ISLAM Malise Ruthven
ISLAMIC HISTORY Adam Silverstein
ISLAMIC LAW Mashood A. Baderin
ISOTOPES Rob Ellam
ITALIAN LITERATURE
    Peter Hainsworth and David Robey
HENRY JAMES Susan L. Mizruchi
JAPANESE LITERATURE Alan Tansman
JESUS Richard Bauckham
JEWISH HISTORY David N. Myers
JEWISH LITERATURE Ilan Stavans
JOURNALISM Ian Hargreaves
JAMES JOYCE Colin MacCabe
JUDAISM Norman Solomon

JUNG Anthony Stevens
THE JURY Renée Lettow Lerner
KABBALAH Joseph Dan
KAFKA Ritchie Robertson
KANT Roger Scruton
KEYNES Robert Skidelsky
KIERKEGAARD Patrick Gardiner
KNOWLEDGE Jennifer Nagel
THE KORAN Michael Cook
KOREA Michael J. Seth
LAKES Warwick F. Vincent
LANDSCAPE ARCHITECTURE
   Ian H. Thompson
LANDSCAPES AND
   GEOMORPHOLOGY
   Andrew Goudie and Heather Viles
LANGUAGES Stephen R. Anderson
LATE ANTIQUITY Gillian Clark
LAW Raymond Wacks
THE LAWS OF THERMODYNAMICS
   Peter Atkins
LEADERSHIP Keith Grint
LEARNING Mark Haselgrove
LEIBNIZ Maria Rosa Antognazza
C. S. LEWIS James Como
LIBERALISM Michael Freeden
LIGHT Ian Walmsley
LINCOLN Allen C. Guelzo
LINGUISTICS Peter Matthews
LITERARY THEORY Jonathan Culler
LOCKE John Dunn
LOGIC Graham Priest
LOVE Ronald de Sousa
MARTIN LUTHER Scott H. Hendrix
MACHIAVELLI Quentin Skinner
MADNESS Andrew Scull
MAGIC Owen Davies
MAGNA CARTA Nicholas Vincent
MAGNETISM Stephen Blundell
MOSES MAIMONIDES Ross Brann
MALTHUS Donald Winch
MAMMALS T. S. Kemp
MANAGEMENT John Hendry
NELSON MANDELA Elleke Boehmer
MAO Delia Davin
MARINE BIOLOGY Philip V. Mladenov
MARKETING
   Kenneth Le Meunier-FitzHugh
THE MARQUIS DE SADE John Phillips
MARTYRDOM Jolyon Mitchell

MARX Peter Singer
MATERIALS Christopher Hall
MATHEMATICAL ANALYSIS
   Richard Earl
MATHEMATICAL FINANCE
   Mark H. A. Davis
MATHEMATICS Timothy Gowers
MATTER Geoff Cottrell
THE MAYA Matthew Restall and
   Amara Solari
MEANING Emma Borg and
   Sarah A. Fisher
THE MEANING OF LIFE Terry Eagleton
MEASUREMENT David Hand
MEDICAL ETHICS Michael Dunn and
   Tony Hope
MEDICAL LAW Charles Foster
MEDIEVAL BRITAIN John Gillingham
   and Ralph A. Griffiths
MEDIEVAL LITERATURE
   Elaine Treharne
MEDIEVAL PHILOSOPHY
   John Marenbon
HERMAN MELVILLE Maurice S. Lee
MEMORY Jonathan K. Foster
METAPHYSICS Stephen Mumford
METHODISM William J. Abraham
THE MEXICAN REVOLUTION
   Alan Knight
MICROBIOLOGY Nicholas P. Money
MICROBIOMES Angela E. Douglas
MICROECONOMICS Avinash Dixit
MICROSCOPY Terence Allen
THE MIDDLE AGES Miri Rubin
MILITARY JUSTICE Eugene R. Fidell
MILITARY STRATEGY
   Antulio J. Echevarria II
JOHN STUART MILL Gregory Claeys
MINERALS David Vaughan
MIRACLES Yujin Nagasawa
MODERN ARCHITECTURE
   Adam Sharr
MODERN ART David Cottington
MODERN BRAZIL Anthony W. Pereira
MODERN CHINA Rana Mitter
MODERN DRAMA
   Kirsten E. Shepherd-Barr
MODERN FRANCE
   Vanessa R. Schwartz
MODERN INDIA Craig Jeffrey

MODERN IRELAND Senia Pašeta
MODERN ITALY Anna Cento Bull
MODERN JAPAN
　Christopher Goto-Jones
MODERN LATIN AMERICAN
　LITERATURE
　Roberto González Echevarría
MODERN WAR Richard English
MODERNISM Christopher Butler
MOLECULAR BIOLOGY Aysha Divan
　and Janice A. Royds
MOLECULES Philip Ball
MONASTICISM Stephen J. Davis
THE MONGOLS Morris Rossabi
MONTAIGNE William M. Hamlin
MOONS David A. Rothery
MORMONISM Richard Lyman Bushman
MOUNTAINS Martin F. Price
MUHAMMAD Jonathan A. C. Brown
MULTICULTURALISM Ali Rattansi
MULTILINGUALISM John C. Maher
MUSIC Nicholas Cook
MUSIC AND TECHNOLOGY
　Mark Katz
MYTH Robert A. Segal
NANOTECHNOLOGY Philip Moriarty
NAPOLEON David A. Bell
THE NAPOLEONIC WARS
　Mike Rapport
NATIONALISM Steven Grosby
NATIVE AMERICAN LITERATURE
　Sean Teuton
NAVIGATION Jim Bennett
NAZI GERMANY Jane Caplan
NEGOTIATION Carrie Menkel-Meadow
NEOLIBERALISM Manfred B. Steger
　and Ravi K. Roy
NETWORKS Guido Caldarelli and
　Michele Catanzaro
THE NEW TESTAMENT
　Luke Timothy Johnson
THE NEW TESTAMENT AS
　LITERATURE Kyle Keefer
NEWTON Robert Iliffe
NIETZSCHE Michael Tanner
NINETEENTH-CENTURY BRITAIN
　Christopher Harvie and
　H. C. G. Matthew
THE NORMAN CONQUEST
　George Garnett

NORTH AMERICAN INDIANS
　Theda Perdue and Michael D. Green
NORTHERN IRELAND
　Marc Mulholland
NOTHING Frank Close
NUCLEAR PHYSICS Frank Close
NUCLEAR POWER Maxwell Irvine
NUCLEAR WEAPONS
　Joseph M. Siracusa
NUMBER THEORY Robin Wilson
NUMBERS Peter M. Higgins
NUTRITION David A. Bender
OBJECTIVITY Stephen Gaukroger
OBSERVATIONAL ASTRONOMY
　Geoff Cottrell
OCEANS Dorrik Stow
THE OLD TESTAMENT
　Michael D. Coogan
ORAL HISTORY Douglas A. Boyd
THE ORCHESTRA D. Kern Holoman
ORGANIC CHEMISTRY
　Graham Patrick
ORGANIZATIONS Mary Jo Hatch
ORGANIZED CRIME
　Georgios A. Antonopoulos and
　Georgios Papanicolaou
ORTHODOX CHRISTIANITY
　A. Edward Siecienski
OVID Llewelyn Morgan
PAGANISM Owen Davies
PAKISTAN Pippa Virdee
THE PALESTINIAN-ISRAELI
　CONFLICT Martin Bunton
PANDEMICS Christian W. McMillen
PARTICLE PHYSICS Frank Close
PAUL E. P. Sanders
IVAN PAVLOV Daniel P. Todes
PEACE Oliver P. Richmond
PENTECOSTALISM William K. Kay
PERCEPTION Brian Rogers
THE PERIODIC TABLE Eric R. Scerri
PHILOSOPHICAL METHOD
　Timothy Williamson
PHILOSOPHY Edward Craig
PHILOSOPHY IN THE ISLAMIC
　WORLD Peter Adamson
PHILOSOPHY OF BIOLOGY
　Samir Okasha
PHILOSOPHY OF LAW
　Raymond Wacks

PHILOSOPHY OF MIND
  Barbara Gail Montero
PHILOSOPHY OF PHYSICS
  David Wallace
PHILOSOPHY OF SCIENCE
  Samir Okasha
PHILOSOPHY OF RELIGION
  Tim Bayne
PHOTOGRAPHY Steve Edwards
PHYSICAL CHEMISTRY Peter Atkins
PHYSICS Sidney Perkowitz
PILGRIMAGE Ian Reader
PLAGUE Paul Slack
PLANETARY SYSTEMS
  Raymond T. Pierrehumbert
PLANETS David A. Rothery
PLANTS Timothy Walker
PLATE TECTONICS Peter Molnar
SYLVIA PLATH Heather Clark
PLATO Julia Annas
POETRY Bernard O'Donoghue
POLITICAL PHILOSOPHY David Miller
POLITICS Kenneth Minogue
POLYGAMY Sarah M. S. Pearsall
POPULISM Cas Mudde and
  Cristóbal Rovira Kaltwasser
POSTCOLONIALISM
  Robert J. C. Young
POSTMODERNISM Christopher Butler
POSTSTRUCTURALISM
  Catherine Belsey
POSTWAR EUROPE Richard Bessel
POVERTY Philip N. Jefferson
PREHISTORY Chris Gosden
PRESOCRATIC PHILOSOPHY
  Catherine Osborne
PRIVACY Raymond Wacks
PROBABILITY John Haigh
PROGRESSIVISM Walter Nugent
PROHIBITION W. J. Rorabaugh
PROJECTS Andrew Davies
PROTESTANTISM Mark A. Noll
MARCEL PROUST Joshua Landy
PSEUDOSCIENCE Michael D. Gordin
PSYCHIATRY Tom Burns
PSYCHOANALYSIS Daniel Pick
PSYCHOLINGUISTICS
  Ferenda Ferreria
PSYCHOLOGY Gillian Butler and
  Freda McManus
PSYCHOLOGY OF MUSIC
  Elizabeth Hellmuth Margulis
PSYCHOPATHY Essi Viding
PSYCHOTHERAPY Tom Burns and
  Eva Burns-Lundgren
PUBLIC ADMINISTRATION
  Stella Z. Theodoulou and Ravi K. Roy
PUBLIC HEALTH Virginia Berridge
PURITANISM Francis J. Bremer
THE QUAKERS Pink Dandelion
QUANTUM THEORY
  John Polkinghorne
RACISM Ali Rattansi
RADIOACTIVITY Claudio Tuniz
RASTAFARI Ennis B. Edmonds
READING Belinda Jack
THE REAGAN REVOLUTION Gil Troy
REALITY Jan Westerhoff
RECONSTRUCTION Allen C. Guelzo
THE REFORMATION Peter Marshall
REFUGEES Gil Loescher
RELATIVITY Russell Stannard
RELIGION Thomas A. Tweed
RELIGION IN AMERICA Timothy Beal
THE RENAISSANCE Jerry Brotton
RENAISSANCE ART
  Geraldine A. Johnson
RENEWABLE ENERGY Nick Jelley
REPTILES T. S. Kemp
REVOLUTIONS Jack A. Goldstone
RHETORIC Richard Toye
RISK Baruch Fischhoff and John Kadvany
RITUAL Barry Stephenson
RIVERS Nick Middleton
ROBOTICS Alan Winfield
ROCKS Jan Zalasiewicz
ROMAN BRITAIN Peter Salway
THE ROMAN EMPIRE
  Christopher Kelly
THE ROMAN REPUBLIC
  David M. Gwynn
ROMANTICISM Michael Ferber
ROUSSEAU Robert Wokler
THE RULE OF LAW Aziz Z. Huq
RUSSELL A. C. Grayling
THE RUSSIAN ECONOMY
  Richard Connolly
RUSSIAN HISTORY Geoffrey Hosking
RUSSIAN LITERATURE Catriona Kelly
RUSSIAN POLITICS Brian D. Taylor

THE RUSSIAN REVOLUTION
  S. A. Smith
SAINTS Simon Yarrow
SAMURAI Michael Wert
SAVANNAS Peter A. Furley
SCEPTICISM Duncan Pritchard
SCHIZOPHRENIA Chris Frith and
  Eve Johnstone
SCHOPENHAUER
  Christopher Janaway
SCIENCE AND RELIGION
  Thomas Dixon and Adam R. Shapiro
SCIENCE FICTION David Seed
THE SCIENTIFIC REVOLUTION
  Lawrence M. Principe
SCOTLAND Rab Houston
SECULARISM Andrew Copson
THE SELF Marya Schechtman
SEXUAL SELECTION Marlene Zuk and
  Leigh W. Simmons
SEXUALITY Véronique Mottier
WILLIAM SHAKESPEARE
  Stanley Wells
SHAKESPEARE'S COMEDIES
  Bart van Es
SHAKESPEARE'S SONNETS AND
  POEMS Jonathan F. S. Post
SHAKESPEARE'S TRAGEDIES
  Stanley Wells
GEORGE BERNARD SHAW
  Christopher Wixson
MARY SHELLEY Charlotte Gordon
THE SHORT STORY Andrew Kahn
SIKHISM Eleanor Nesbitt
SILENT FILM Donna Kornhaber
THE SILK ROAD James A. Millward
SLANG Jonathon Green
SLEEP Steven W. Lockley and
  Russell G. Foster
SMELL Matthew Cobb
ADAM SMITH Christopher J. Berry
SOCIAL AND CULTURAL
  ANTHROPOLOGY
  John Monaghan and Peter Just
SOCIALISM Michael Newman
SOCIAL PSYCHOLOGY Richard J. Crisp
SOCIAL SCIENCE Alexander Betts
SOCIAL WORK Sally Holland and
  Jonathan Scourfield
SOCIOLINGUISTICS John Edwards
SOCIOLOGY Steve Bruce
SOCRATES C. C. W. Taylor
SOFT MATTER Tom McLeish
SOPHOCLES Edith Hall
SOUND Mike Goldsmith
SOUTHEAST ASIA James R. Rush
THE SOVIET UNION Stephen Lovell
THE SPANISH CIVIL WAR
  Helen Graham
SPANISH LITERATURE Jo Labanyi
THE SPARTANS Andrew J. Bayliss
SPINOZA Roger Scruton
SPIRITUALITY Philip Sheldrake
SPORT Mike Cronin
STARS Andrew King
STATISTICS David J. Hand
STEM CELLS Jonathan Slack
STOICISM Brad Inwood
STRUCTURAL ENGINEERING
  David Blockley
STUART BRITAIN John Morrill
SUBURBS Carl Abbott
THE SUN Philip Judge
SUPERCONDUCTIVITY
  Stephen Blundell
SUPERSTITION Stuart Vyse
SURVEILLANCE David Lyon
SUSTAINABILITY Saleem Ali
SYMBIOSIS Nancy A. Moran
SYMMETRY Ian Stewart
SYNAESTHESIA Julia Simner
SYNTHETIC BIOLOGY Jamie A. Davies
SYSTEMS BIOLOGY Eberhard O. Voit
TAXATION Stephen Smith
TEETH Peter S. Ungar
TERRORISM Charles Townshend
THEATRE Marvin Carlson
THEOLOGY David F. Ford
THINKING AND REASONING
  Jonathan St B. T. Evans
HENRY DAVID THOREAU
  Lawrence Buell
THOUGHT Tim Bayne
THUCYDIDES Jennifer T. Roberts
TIBETAN BUDDHISM
  Matthew T. Kapstein
TIDES David George Bowers and
  Emyr Martyn Roberts
TIME Jenann Ismael
TOCQUEVILLE Harvey C. Mansfield

TOLERATION Andrew Murphy
J. R. R. TOLKIEN Matthew Townend
LEO TOLSTOY Liza Knapp
TOPOLOGY Richard Earl
TRAGEDY Adrian Poole
TRANSLATION Matthew Reynolds
THE TREATY OF VERSAILLES
    Michael S. Neiberg
TRIGONOMETRY
    Glen Van Brummelen
THE TROJAN WAR Eric H. Cline
ANTHONY TROLLOPE Dinah Birch
TRUST Katherine Hawley
THE TUDORS John Guy
TWENTIETH-CENTURY BRITAIN
    Kenneth O. Morgan
TYPOGRAPHY Paul Luna
THE UNITED NATIONS
    Jussi M. Hanhimäki
UNIVERSITIES AND COLLEGES
    David Palfreyman and Paul Temple
THE U.S. CIVIL WAR Louis P. Masur
THE U.S. CONGRESS Donald A. Ritchie
THE U.S. CONSTITUTION
    David J. Bodenhamer
THE U.S. SUPREME COURT
    Linda Greenhouse
UTILITARIANISM
    Katarzyna de Lazari-Radek and
    Peter Singer
UTOPIANISM Lyman Tower Sargent
VATICAN II Shaun Blanchard and
    Stephen Bullivant
VETERINARY SCIENCE James Yeates
THE VICTORIANS Martin Hewitt
THE VIKINGS Julian D. Richards
VIOLENCE Philip Dwyer
THE VIRGIN MARY
    Mary Joan Winn Leith
THE VIRTUES Craig A. Boyd and
    Kevin Timpe
VIRUSES Dorothy H. Crawford
VOLCANOES Michael J. Branney and
    Jan Zalasiewicz
VOLTAIRE Nicholas Cronk
WAR AND RELIGION Jolyon Mitchell
    and Joshua Rey
WAR AND TECHNOLOGY
    Alex Roland
WATER John Finney
WAVES Mike Goldsmith
WEATHER Storm Dunlop
SIMONE WEIL
    A. Rebecca Rozelle-Stone
THE WELFARE STATE David Garland
WITCHCRAFT Malcolm Gaskill
WITTGENSTEIN A. C. Grayling
WORK Stephen Fineman
WORLD MUSIC Philip Bohlman
WORLD MYTHOLOGY
    David Leeming
THE WORLD TRADE
    ORGANIZATION Amrita Narlikar
WORLD WAR II Gerhard L. Weinberg
WRITING AND SCRIPT
    Andrew Robinson
ZIONISM Michael Stanislawski
ÉMILE ZOLA Brian Nelson

Available soon:

ADMINISTRATIVE LAW
    Stephen Thomson

EVOLUTIONARY PSYCHOLOGY
    Maryanne Fisher and T. Joel Wade

For more information visit our website

www.oup.com/vsi/

Maurice S. Lee

HERMAN MELVILLE

A Very Short Introduction

OXFORD
UNIVERSITY PRESS

Oxford University Press is a department of the University of Oxford.
It furthers the University's objective of excellence in research, scholarship,
and education by publishing worldwide. Oxford is a registered trade mark of
Oxford University Press in the UK and in certain other countries.

Published in the United States of America by Oxford University Press
198 Madison Avenue, New York, NY 10016, United States of America.

© Oxford University Press 2025

All rights reserved. No part of this publication may be reproduced, stored in a retrieval system,
transmitted, used for text and data mining, or used for training artificial intelligence, in any form or
by any means, without the prior permission in writing of Oxford University Press, or as expressly
permitted by law, by license or under terms agreed with the appropriate reprographics rights
organization. Inquiries concerning reproduction outside the scope of the above should be sent
to the Rights Department, Oxford University Press, at the address above.

You must not circulate this work in any other form
and you must impose this same condition on any acquirer.

Library of Congress Cataloging-in-Publication Data
Names: Lee, Maurice S. author
Title: Herman Melville : a very short introduction / Maurice S. Lee.
Description: New York, NY : Oxford University Press, 2025. |
Series: A very short introduction | Includes bibliographical references and index.
Identifiers: LCCN 2025019943 (print) | LCCN 2025019944 (ebook) |
ISBN 9780197753057 paperback | ISBN 9780197753071 epub
Subjects: LCSH: Melville, Herman, 1819–1891 | Melville, Herman,
1819–1891—Criticism and interpretation | Novelists, American—
19th century—Biography | LCGFT: Biographies | Literary criticism
Classification: LCC PS2386 .L35 2025 (print) | LCC PS2386 (ebook) |
DDC 813/.3 [B]—dc23/eng/20250512
LC record available at https://lccn.loc.gov/2025019943
LC ebook record available at https://lccn.loc.gov/2025019944

DOI: 10.1093/9780197753088.001.0001

Printed by Integrated Books International, United States of America

The manufacturer's authorized representative in the EU for product safety is
Oxford University Press España S.A. of Parque Empresarial San Fernando de Henares,
Avenida de Castilla, 2 – 28830 Madrid (www.oup.es/en or product.safety@oup.com).
OUP España S.A. also acts as importer into Spain of products made by the manufacturer.

The manufacturer's authorised representative in the EU for product safety is Oxford University Press España S.A. of El Parque Empresarial
San Fernando de Henares, Avenida de Castilla, 2 – 28830 Madrid (www.oup.es/en or product.safety@oup.com). OUP España S.A. also acts as
importer into Spain of products made by the manufacturer.

Contents

List of illustrations xvii

Works frequently cited in this volume xix

More than *Moby-Dick* xxi

1 A brief biography 1

2 Truth, sex, and empire: The Pacific Island novels 16

3 A moving world: *Redburn* and *White-Jacket* 30

4 Four reasons for going to sea in *Moby-Dick* 44

5 Antagonisms: *Pierre*, *Israel Potter*, and *The Confidence-Man* 65

6 Melville's magazine fiction 79

7 Pushed and pulled to poetry 95

A ragged conclusion: *Billy Budd* 110

References 119

Further reading 125

Index 129

List of illustrations

1 Photograph of Herman Melville by Rodney Dewey, 1861 **2**
   With permission of the Berkshire Athenaeum, Pittsfield, Massachusetts

2 Oil painting of Herman Melville by Joseph Eaton, 1870 **3**
   With permission of the Houghton Library, Harvard University

3 Oil painting of Maria Gansevoort Melvill by Ezra Ames, ca. 1820 **6**
   With permission of the Berkshire Athenaeum, Pittsfield, Massachusetts

4 Photograph of Elizabeth Shaw Melville, ca. 1847 **11**
   With permission of the Berkshire Athenaeum, Pittsfield, Massachusetts

5 John Bachmann, "Birds' Eye View of Manhattan and Brooklyn" (1851) **12**
   Lithograph from Library of Congress (PAGA 7, no. 4370)

6 Melville Letter to Nathaniel Hawthorne, August 13, 1852 **13**
   MS Am 188 (173), Houghton Library, Harvard University

7 Map of the Marquesas Islands **19**
   Engraving from Herman Melville's *Narrative of a Four Months Residence among the Natives of a Valley of the Marquesas Islands* (London: John Murray, 1846)

8 "Boats Attacking Whales" **50**
   Engraving from Thomas Beal's *The Natural History of the Sperm Whale* (London: John Van Voorst, 1839)

9 "Apparatus Used in the Whale Fishery" **51**
   Engraving from William Scoresby's *An Account of the Arctic Regions*, Vol. 2 (Edinburgh: Archibald Constable and Co., 1820)

10 Final page of *Billy Budd* manuscript **116**
   MS Am 188 (363), Houghton Library, Harvard University

Works frequently cited in this volume

Herman Melville, *Complete Poems: Battle-Pieces and Aspects of War; Clarel: A Poem and Pilgrimage in the Holy Land; John Marr and Other Sailors with Some Sea-Pieces; Timoleon Etc.; Weeds and Wildings Chiefly: with A Rose or Two; Parthenope; Uncollected Poetry and Prose-and-Verse*, ed. Hershel Parker (New York: Library of America, 2019).

Herman Melville, *Pierre: or, The Ambiguities; Israel Potter: His Fifty Years of Exile; The Piazza Tales; The Confidence-Man: His Masquerade; Uncollected Prose; Billy Budd, Sailor: (An Inside Narrative)* (New York: Library of America, 1985).

Herman Melville, *Redburn: His First Voyage; White-Jacket: or The World in a Man-of-War; Moby-Dick: or, The Whale* (New York: Library of America, 1983).

Herman Melville, *Typee: A Peep at Polynesian Life; Omoo: A Narrative of Adventures in the South Seas; Mardi: and A Voyage Thither* (New York: Library of America, 1982).

Herman Melville, *The Writings of Herman Melville: Correspondence*, ed. Lynn Horth (Evanston and Chicago: Northwestern University Press and the Newberry Library, 1993).

More than *Moby-Dick*

Herman Melville is among a handful of people who can be considered America's greatest writer. Best known for *Moby-Dick*, Melville's achievements range from popular novels and experimental fiction to powerful poetry. His works are tragic and funny, impassioned and ironic, attuned to the details of everyday life, and dedicated to philosophical and religious seeking. Melville engaged pressing issues of his day, from economic inequality and the American slavery crisis to the rise of science and the fragility of democracy. He also dwelled on timeless questions about loneliness and intimacy, the responsibilities we owe others, the limits of our knowledge and agency, and the place of human beings in the cosmos. Melville is a thinker who writes not only about everything, but about the relations between everything and everything else. His language swings between high eloquence and street speech, familiar genres and original concoctions. Though his writing is immensely influential today, it remains profoundly strange.

Melville's life was dramatic, and his career was improbable. He was born into privilege in 1819; fell into poverty as an adolescent; hunted whales and lived with the Tai Pī people of Polynesia; served in the United States Navy; skyrocketed to fame as a novelist; ruined his career by questioning religious, sexual, political, and artistic orthodoxies; reinvented himself as a poet during the Civil War; and died in 1891 in relative obscurity just as readers began to recognize his genius. The scope and diversity of Melville's writings reflect a life of restless ambition. There is much to Melville, and this *Very Short Introduction* should help readers explore the richness of his work.

Chapter 1
A brief biography

We have six portraits of Herman Melville, and in none of them is he smiling. In three of them, he looks directly at the viewer with self-possessed curiosity. It's the gaze of a writer more interested in observing others than in sharing truths about himself. Two of the portraits are profiles of Melville, his averted face and darkened eyes suggesting someone lost in thought. And one of his portraits, a photograph from 1861, shows him facing the camera but glancing just slightly to the side. With arms crossed tightly against his body, it looks as if he has just broken off or is refusing to make eye contact. In all six portraits, Melville's dress is formal but not fancy, and there are none of the ornaments, furnishings, or books that sometimes appear in nineteenth-century portraits to signal social status or personal commitments. The viewer has little choice but to focus on Melville's face—thick beard, straight nose, high cheekbones, blue eyes, and (until his later years) dark hair swept back over a prominent forehead. When he became famous in his late twenties, people described him as handsome and mysterious. Sophia Hawthorne, Nathaniel's wife, said of Melville's gaze, "It is a strange, lazy glance, but with a power in it quite unique. It does not seem to penetrate through you, but to take you into itself."

Melville is one of America's most famous writers, but despite a century of dedicated scholarship, much of his life remains elusive.

1. Herman Melville in 1861. Photograph taken by Rodney Dewey when Melville was living in Pittsfield, Massachusetts.

2. **Herman Melville in 1870. Oil on canvas portrait by Joseph Eaton.**

He did not leave extensive private records such as letters and journals, and, as his portraits and many of his characters suggest, he was often a solitary man. Parts of his biography can be inferred from his fiction and poetry, which reflect the wide experience and unbounded thought of an unsettled iconoclast. Yet as revealing as Melville's literature can be, it raises as many questions as answers, leading finally to what Andrew Delbanco has called "the edge of his inner life." A point that many of Melville's writings make is that people never really understand each other.

We know more about Melville's public career, which makes for a dramatic story of disaster, recovery, self-sabotage, and redemption. Born in 1819 in New York City, the young Melville enjoyed many advantages. His grandfather from the Scottish side of the family, Thomas Melvill, graduated from Princeton College, participated in the Boston Tea Party, served as a major during the Revolutionary War, and held appointments overseeing the Port of Boston. Melville's maternal grandfather, Peter Gansevoort, came from a prominent Dutch family in New York and led the American victory over British, Mohawk, and Seneca forces at the Battle of Fort Stanwix. If one squints, Gilbert Stuart's portrait of General Gansevoort looks like Stuart's famous painting of George Washington. That Melville's older brother was named Gansevoort and that Melville would name his second child Stanwix indicate how seriously he and his family regarded their place in US history. The unfulfilled ideals of the Revolution—liberty, equality, and democracy—are the subject of many Melville writings.

Melville's family retained their elevated station at the start of the nineteenth century. His father, Allan Melvill, was a merchant in Manhattan who had traveled through Europe, spoke fluent French, and imported luxury goods. He married Maria Gansevoort, who as a child of the General and a daughter of wealth was educated in the rigors of Dutch Calvinism and the pleasures of music and dance. Melville's parents dressed well, had multiple servants, and sent their sons to private academies. The Revolution had its egalitarian ideals, but Melville's family, especially through its Gansevoort lineage, was part of America's elite.

Unfortunately, Allan was better at consuming than selling luxury goods. In 1830 he absconded with the family to Albany to dodge creditors who were threatening prosecution at a time when debtors' prisons still existed in America. Allan sent desperate letters to his father and in-laws while struggling to keep up appearances. In 1832 he caught pneumonia and died raving from a fever, leaving Maria and her eight children with few assets and no income.

Such turns of fortune were not unusual in an era of upward and downward mobility. Having concluded his tour of the United States one month after Allan's death, the French intellectual Alexis de Tocqueville wrote of America: "[W]ealth circulates with an astonishing speed and experience shows that rarely do two succeeding generations benefit from its favors." Born one year before Melville and quoting from Shakespeare, Karl Marx expressed a similar view when charging that under the "everlasting uncertainty" of capitalism, "[a]ll that is solid melts into air."

Melville was twelve when his father died—old enough to understand the damage to his prospects but too young to do much about it. His family depended on relatives for support as they shuttled between New York and Massachusetts. They were fortunate not to slip into hunger and homelessness, but the price was tribulation and shame. Not long after her husband's death, the strong-willed but beleaguered Maria added an "e" to her last name.

The death of his father began Melville's search for a career and, more existentially, a place in the world. Unable to consistently continue his education, he ran errands for a bank (a job arranged through relatives), worked at a clothing store (run by his brother Gansevoort), lived on a Massachusetts farm (owned by an uncle), and taught school (while boarding with the parents of his pupils). Melville was white, somewhat educated, and had family connections, but he entered adulthood during an unpropitious time. Spurred by land speculation, unregulated banks, and Andrew Jackson's monetary policies, the Panic of 1837 brought credit shortages and unemployment that would depress the US

5

3. Maria Gansevoort Melvill around 1820, one year after the birth of Herman. After the bankruptcy and death of her husband, Maria added an "e" to her last name. Oil on canvas portrait by Ezra Ames.

economy for nearly a decade. Melville was not alone in his vocational struggles, nor was he the only young American to recognize that in a nation that valorized self-reliance and saw itself as a land of opportunity, failure and success were often determined by forces beyond one's control.

In 1839 the nineteen-year-old Melville joined a merchant ship sailing between New York and Liverpool, marking his entrance into a maritime industry that enriched shipowners and merchants, offered careers to captains and mates, and paid common sailors low wages for dangerous work. We know little about Melville's inaugural voyage, though his novel *Redburn* (1849) tells the story of a well-bred, fatherless youth learning hard lessons as a sailor. After returning from Liverpool, Melville taught at another school (which went bankrupt), studied surveying and engineering (without finding employment in the field), and traveled to Illinois (where he could not land a job). Melville's life seemed a disappointing failure to launch when he signed on to a whaling voyage. He may have done so out of economic necessity, a desire for adventure, or a need to prove himself to (or distance himself from) his family. Whatever the reasons, his decision proved to be the most momentous of his life.

Whaling cruises often lasted for years, with crew members earning a share of whale oil, a major commodity before the decimation of whale populations and the rise of the petroleum industry. Poorly managed or unlucky voyages could leave a sailor with little compensation. Crews also risked storms and shipwrecks in remote waters as they pursued their quarry in light, thirty-foot-long boats in the hope of harpooning a massive whale and being dragged behind it until it tired. Bad food, disease, and abusive superiors made the life even more difficult, but despite—and because of—its many hardships, whaling was often romanticized. It allowed young men to test their courage and broaden their experience, throwing together laborers of different nations, races, ethnicities, religions, languages, and sexual practices. At the center of an extractive global industry where fortunes were made and lives lost, whaling vessels were among the most dangerous and diverse places in the nineteenth century. As such, they offered opportunities for living beyond and critiquing social norms.

Melville's whaling voyage was especially exciting, almost unbelievably so. He shipped from New Bedford, Massachusetts, in 1841, sailing around Cape Horn and up the coast of South America to the whaling grounds of the Pacific. When his ship stopped at Nuku Hiva in the Marquesas Islands, he jumped ship and lived among the Tai Pī people, who were rumored to be cannibals. After a month, Melville signed on to an Australian whaler, joined a group of sailors who refused to work for their alcoholic first mate, and for this was imprisoned for two weeks in Tahiti before walking away from the unguarded jail. From there Melville moved to a neighboring island (where he farmed sweet potatoes), sailed with another whaler (this one from Nantucket), and again abandoned ship (this time in Hawaii, where he was outraged by the degrading influence of Westerners on indigenous culture). Eventually he joined a US Naval frigate, serving for fourteen months before the ship returned to Boston in 1844. Melville had been gone for nearly four years, and it must have felt like a lifetime.

Nothing in Melville's early years compared to his wild experiences at sea, which shaped his outlook on the world and launched an unlikely literary career. In his half-a-dozen years of formal schooling, Melville had been a largely unexceptional student with poor spelling and bad handwriting. As a teenager, he joined debating societies and availed himself of books, though Gansevoort was the better speaker and a more meticulous reader. Melville published a few pieces in local newspapers, and at sea he had access to small libraries, as well as to sailors who knew books and spun yarns. But it was not until he had his own sea stories to tell—and had practiced them on shipmates, family, and friends—that he took up writing in a serious way.

Within a year of his return to America, Melville finished *Typee* (1846), an exotic narrative about a young sailor who abandons his ship in the Marquesas Islands. The American publishing house Harper and Brothers rejected Melville's manuscript, but Gansevoort, who was serving as a diplomat in England, succeeded in placing the book with John Murray. *Typee* was well received in Britain and America—enjoyed by some reviewers as a thrilling adventure, censured by others for criticizing Christian missionaries, and both enjoyed and censured for its titillating descriptions of sexual freedoms in the South Seas. With controversies surrounding the book and Melville embracing his reputation as a rough-hewn tar, he was, in Hershel Parker's words, "the first American author to become a sex symbol."

Melville's emergence as a professional writer came at a time when advances in print technology, distribution, and literacy rapidly expanded the market for books. Other authors born within a decade of Melville—including Charles Dickens, Edgar Allan Poe, Margaret Fuller, Harriet Beecher Stowe, and Fanny Fern—responded to declines in their economic status by trying to write their way to financial security. With *Typee*, Melville launched a career and even a personal brand, publishing four additional sea novels within the next four years. Such production reflects his passion and work ethic, as well as the desperate economics of authorship. In the mid-nineteenth century, aspiring writers crowded the marketplace, readers were inundated with texts, and the lack of an international copyright law made it more profitable for American publishers to pirate British books than adequately pay domestic authors.

Nonetheless, Melville made his way in the American literary scene. He began his career in New York City, which grew from 300,000 to 500,000 people between 1840 and 1850 and was fast becoming the center of American publishing. Though never a dedicated networker or entrepreneur, Melville became associated with the Young America movement, a group of US writers and editors committed to building a national literary tradition independent of British influence. On the heels of *Typee*, Melville published *Omoo* (1847), a much anticipated and commercially successful sequel. His next book, the fantastical allegory

Mardi (1849), failed both critically and financially, though Melville righted the ship with *Redburn* and *White-Jacket* (1850), which he described in a letter as "two *jobs*, which I have done for money—being forced to it, as other men are to sawing wood."

Melville visited Britain and read extensively during this period, particularly admiring the eloquence and dense styles of Shakespeare, Milton, Thomas Browne, and the King James Bible. His maturing prose shows a wealth of aesthetic influences, explicit borrowings, and allusive echoes, even as he crafted a distinctive literary voice marked by sweeping rhythms and startling locutions. Melville aspired to artistic originality, though he also felt financial pressures to please his readers with familiar ideas and forms.

The tension became acute as his family responsibilities grew alongside his literary ambitions. Gansevoort died in 1846, leaving Melville the primary earner in the family. In 1847 he married Elizabeth Shaw, daughter of Lemuel Shaw, the chief justice of the Massachusetts Supreme Court and an old friend of Allan Melvill. Lizzie (as she was known) was a supportive spouse who copied and helped edit Melville's manuscripts. She also endured his volatile moods and, as Elizabeth Renker has argued, instances of physical abuse. With the help of Lizzie's father, the couple purchased a home in Manhattan and began having children—Malcolm (born in 1849), Stanwix (1851), Elizabeth (1853), and Frances (1855). After fifteen years of searching for a place in the world in the wake of his father's death, Melville had a profession, home, and family of his own.

And yet, like his father, he continued to take risks. In 1850 he purchased a farm in the Berkshires of Massachusetts, where he and his family lived for the next thirteen years. It strained their already tenuous finances but brought Melville close to Nathaniel Hawthorne, with whom he formed an intense, short-lived relationship that, based on Melville's passionate letters, was

4. Elizabeth Shaw Melville at the age of twenty-five. Photograph taken in 1847, the year she married Herman.

artistically inspiring and sexually charged. Hawthorne's achievements motivated Melville to pursue his own literary vision, even at great personal cost. The result was *Moby-Dick* (1851), a whaling adventure turned philosophical, religious, and political epic that is awesome in every sense of the word. Melville recognized the book's greatness but was not optimistic about its

5. New York City, where Melville spent most of his life. Lithograph from 1851 by John Bachmann.

professional success, writing to Hawthorne: "Dollars damn me.... What I feel most moved to write, that is banned,—it will not pay. Yet, altogether, write the *other* way I cannot." He was right insofar as *Moby-Dick* was met with mixed reviews and middling sales.

The book also marks an inflection point in the trajectory of Melville's career.

In the decade following *Moby-Dick*, Melville published three novels and sixteen short stories—almost none of them about the sea, and many expressing profound disillusionment. *Pierre* (1852), a book that demolishes conventions of marriage and sex while disparaging reviewers and publishers, was predictably condemned to the point that some commenters called for a boycott of Melville. After this act of professional self-sabotage, Melville turned to magazine fiction, writing tales critical of Christianity, American

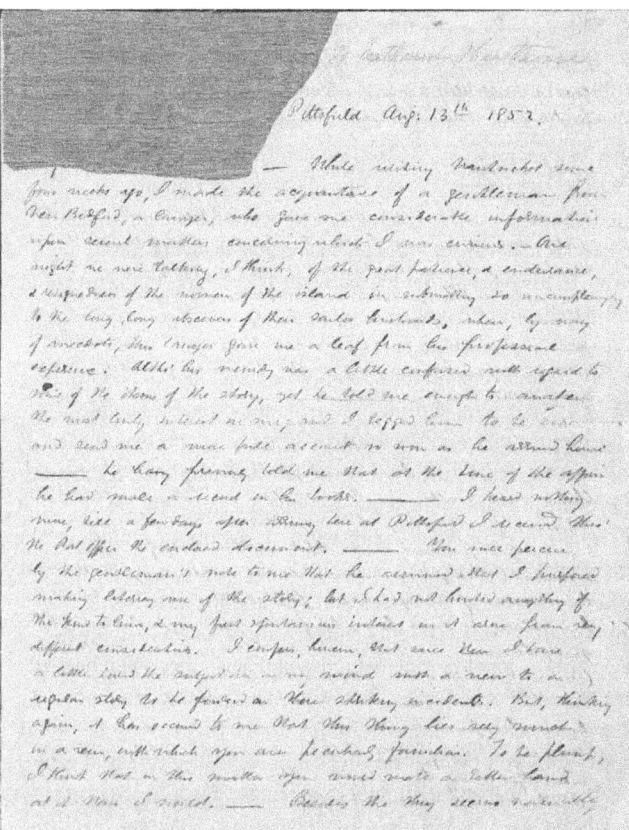

6. Melville to Nathaniel Hawthorne on August 13, 1852. Melville's letters to Hawthorne are passionate, though the friendship later cooled.

exceptionalism, capitalism, imperialism, and slavery. Along the way, his historical novel *Israel Potter* (1855) satirized facile celebrations of the American Revolution, while *The Confidence-Man* (1857) teased readers with unknowable characters and unsolvable philosophical puzzles.

Melville's earlier books often softened their iconoclasm with adventure, whimsy, and humor. His writings after *Moby-Dick* are brilliant but also embittered and enigmatic, as his popularity plummeted, his debts grew, his treatment of his family worsened, and his in-laws worried about his sanity. Borrowing against Lizzie's inheritance, in 1856 Melville took a six-month Mediterranean trip in the hope of recovering his mental health. When Hawthorne met him on a Liverpool beach that year, he wrote in his journal that his erstwhile friend had "made up his mind to be annihilated."

Melville would encounter other personal challenges—continuing financial struggles, chronic back pain, the probable suicide of Malcolm in 1867, and the death of Stanwix from tuberculosis in 1886. At the end of the Civil War, Melville became a US Customs inspector in Manhattan, a low-ranking bureaucratic position that he would hold for twenty years without earning a promotion. The job freed Melville from depending on his writing for income, and inheritances in the 1880s enabled him and Lizzie to live comfortably. Financial independence also allowed Melville to leave professional writing behind, so much so that when he died in 1891, the few obituaries that noticed his passing remembered him as the author of sea adventures from half a century before. It makes for a compelling tragedy: shunned by a culture that could not handle his truths, the suffering genius slips into obscurity. Raymond Weaver, Melville's first biographer, called the last three decades of his life a "Long Quietus."

Yet Melville did not abandon writing after losing his public standing in the 1850s. He turned to poetry, including the powerful collection *Battle-Pieces* (1866), which meditates on the ambiguities and grief of the American Civil War. Ten years later, he published *Clarel* (1876), a monumental poem that traces faith and doubt among a party of travelers in Palestine. As he entered his seventies, Melville privately printed two more books of verse, and at his death left a manuscript of *Billy Budd*, one of his most important works.

The nineteenth-century novelist William Dean Howells once wrote, "What the American public wants . . . is a tragedy with a happy ending." Melville's life can fit this bill, for after his upended adolescence, transient twenties, surprising rise as an author, and self-inflicted professional decline, a new generation of readers began rediscovering his work in the years around his passing. Since the revival of Melville among scholars in the 1920s, his prominence has increased with the rise of American literature as an academic and popular subject. No American author is regarded more highly. No book is more celebrated than *Moby-Dick*. No matter what a reader tends to value—stirring plots, audacious style, psychological complexity, religious and philosophical questing, or critiques of identity, power, and justice—Melville's writings remain immensely rewarding. His life is fascinating in and of itself, and his biography is a crucial context for his work. But what makes Melville most remarkable is his literature, which is what we turn to next.

Chapter 2
Truth, sex, and empire: The Pacific Island novels

A rebel, a neglected genius, a writer too far ahead of his time—Melville's posthumous reputation has largely rested on the uncompromising originality of his mature fiction, above all *Moby-Dick* (1851). Yet Melville's best-known book during his life was his first and was not especially groundbreaking. *Typee* (1846) works slyly within literary traditions, only hinting at the radical intellectual and aesthetic possibilities that Melville would later explore. The book begins a trio of Pacific Island novels by Melville that includes *Omoo* (1847) and *Mardi* (1849). Of the three, *Typee* is the best introduction, not only to Melville's thematic interests and emergence as an author, but also to the literary and social contexts he navigated throughout his career. For readers introducing themselves to Melville's work, there are good reasons to begin at the start.

Written from the perspective of a sailor we know only as Tommo, *Typee* traces how Tommo and his friend Toby abandon their whaling ship for the interior of Nuku Hiva island, a region inhabited by the supposedly cannibalistic Typee, who treat the pair with surprising generosity. Tommo lives with Marheyo and his son Kory-Kory, while he meets the multilingual Polynesian Marnoo and dallies with the beautiful Fayaway. Tommo describes Typee culture in detail as he vacillates between enjoying his idyllic life and suspecting that he is actually a captive soon to be tattooed or eaten. After Toby disappears and Tommo decides that his hosts are in fact cannibals, he flees to join the crew of an Australian whaler, striking a Typee leader with a boathook during his escape.

Typee appealed to its audience in two different and not always compatible ways: as a suspenseful, improbable adventure, and as a supposedly accurate account of an exotic culture. Walt Whitman, a little-known journalist at the time, called *Typee* "a most readable book." As with much commercially successful media, *Typee* met the expectations of its audience by adopting familiar conventions. A critical question is how closely Melville hews to the genre of South Sea fiction, for *Typee* is a crowd-pleasing effort that struggled to please everyone, especially after it sparked three controversies.

Truth

The first controversy involved a seemingly simple question: Was *Typee* fictional or true? Today, the book seems clearly a novel (or what was termed a *romance* in the nineteenth century). Melville take artistic liberties with his personal history and Tai Pī culture, while his account of wild adventures on a tropic island joins a tradition of South Sea novels that includes Edgar Allan Poe's *Narrative of Arthur Gordon Pym* (1838), Frederick Marryat's *Masterman Ready* (1841), and James Fenimore Cooper's *The Crater* (1847)—all fictional narratives that were received as such.

But *Typee* was harder for Melville's contemporaries to assess. First published in Britain as part of a travel writing series, the book includes unlikely-but-believable incidents, ethnographic details, historical contexts, and references to nonfictional books on Polynesia. It thus presented itself as true, though Melville's publisher worried—quite correctly, it turned out—that some readers would doubt its veracity. Melville accordingly added more facts and adjusted his style to sound more like that of a common sailor. The revised book was published in the United States as

Typee: A Peep at Polynesian Life, and Melville wrote in a preface that he hoped the story's "unvarnished truth" would "gain for him the confidence of his readers." Melville would later become a more defiant writer, but at the start of his career he was willing to accommodate, at least superficially, the expectations of his audience. The challenge was that their expectations varied, as some reviewers judged *Typee* as a fiction, while others worried about Melville's authenticity, and still others did both at once. The multiple editions of the book—John Bryant calls *Typee* a "fluid text"—reflect how Melville was buffeted by competing demands for romance and accuracy. Regaling family and friends with tall tales of the sea turned out to be easier than becoming an author.

As if anticipating such problems, *Typee* is a subtly self-aware book that plays with distinctions between fiction and truth. Melville—or more accurately, Tommo—exults before even arriving at Nuku Hiva:

> The Marquesas! What strange visions of outlandish things does the very name spirit up! Naked houris—cannibal banquets—groves of cocoa-nut—coral reefs—tattooed chiefs—and bamboo temples; sunny valleys planted with bread-fruit-trees—carved canoes dancing on the flashing blue waters—savage woodlands guarded by horrible idols—*heathenish rites and human sacrifices*.

With italics and exclamation points implying an imagination run amok, what Tommo calls his "strangely jumbled expectations" show that he has internalized exotic tropes endemic to South Sea fiction. When he later chastises readers of Marryat and mocks "adventurous youths who abandon vessels in romantic islands," he suggests that his firsthand experiences on Nuku Hiva have disabused him of such fantasies.

And yet *Typee* is not simply a narrative of romance giving way to reality. Tommo's time on Nuku Hiva ends up fulfilling his

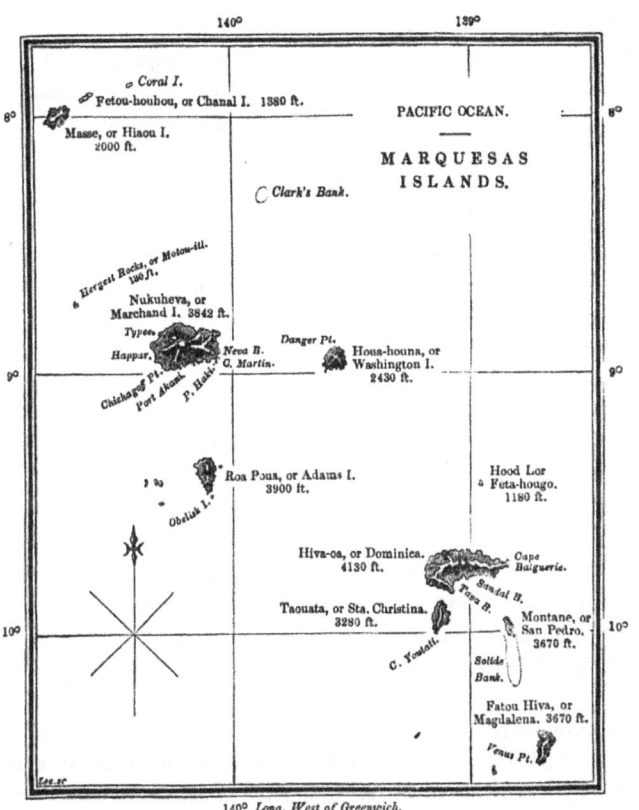

7. The Marquesas Islands from Melville's *Narrative of a Four Months Residence among the Natives of a Valley of the Marquesas Islands* (1846), later retitled *Typee*.

expectations, even as it shows how his experiences are colored by his jumbled preconceptions. Struggling with linguistic and cultural barriers that undermine his reliability, and (as Sigmund and Anna Freud might argue) projecting his forbidden thoughts onto the Typee people, Tommo's interpretations of his hosts' behavior reflect his own desires and fears.

Most dramatically, rumors of cannibalism haunt Tommo's imagination. Anthropophagy had long been a topic of racist speculation in European writings about Oceania and beyond, and James Cook famously reported cannibalism by the Māori people before being killed by Hawaiians in 1779 (and assumed to be eaten by them). When Tommo sees Typee warriors returning from battle bearing a load covered with bloody leaves, he surmises—and then assumes—that it is the body of an enemy that they will eat. Yet uncertainty lingers when Tommo acknowledges that he bases his inferences on limited observations and the explanations that Kory-Kory provides through gestures and the small vocabulary they share. Tommo later sees a "slight glimpse" of what he thinks are human bones, which he takes as unequivocal proof of cannibalism. This is not to say that he is mistaken, for the accuracy of his apprehensions (in both senses of the word) are never confirmed or denied. For Geoffrey Sanborn, *Typee* asks its readers to maintain two disparate lines of thought—one that seeks to identify the truth of Typee practices, and one that recognizes how subjective and cultural misunderstandings inevitably complicate such efforts.

In accord with the jumbled expectations of its audience, *Typee* blurs the boundaries between fiction and nonfiction, foregrounds the interplay between imagination and reality, and suggests that experience is never free from prejudices generated by, among other things, books. It is not simply that Tommo is an unreliable narrator. The very nature of cross-cultural encounters makes it hard to tell the unvarnished truth, especially about people who are frequently stereotyped. *Typee*'s originality may lie in its suggestion that original—that is, unmediated—experience is impossible. The problem is that Melville simultaneously insisted on the authenticity of *Typee*, which encouraged the public to conflate him with the narrator Tommo, thus exacerbating a second controversy.

Sex

When Tommo's ship, the *Dolly*, arrives in Nuku Hiva Harbor, a group of naked Indigenous women swim out and mingle promiscuously with the sailors. Tommo dwells on their beautiful bodies before demurring, "[T]here is an abandoned voluptuousness in their character which I dare not describe." Yet dare he does, at least to some degree: "Our ship was now wholly given up to every species of riot and debauchery. Not the feeblest barrier was interposed between the unholy passions of the crew and their unlimited gratification." In Melville's carefully constructed scene, Tommo unabashedly admires the women, but once the sexual activity begins, he shifts from a first- to third-person perspective, thereby exempting himself from the behavior of the crew.

Such plausible deniability mattered, given Melville's close association with Tommo. *Typee* earned Melville the reputation of a Byronic, bad-boy author, but to implicate himself in any debauchery would compromise his reputation in a book read by his Calvinist mother, dedicated to his soon-to-be father-in-law, reviewed by an influential Protestant press, and consumed by a Christian public. In the *Dolly* scene, Melville presents his narrator—and himself—as simultaneously sensual and upstanding.

The Victorian age is often taken to deny sexual desire, but the period was actually preoccupied with sex, if only to more strenuously regulate it. On the one hand, lawmakers tightened sexual restrictions, physicians constructed sexual norms, conduct manuals enforced chaste behavior, and constraints appeared in everyday life—from body-controlling fashions and gender-segregated spaces to anti-masturbation tracts and diets intended to limit libido. On the other hand, sex. People, of course, were not bound by the proscriptions of heterosexuality, marriage, and reproduction. Gay and lesbian subcultures existed, even if they were largely unrecognized. Queer literary works, some more coded than others, represented same-sex desire and gender nonconformity with degrees of disapproval, sympathy, and ambivalence. As diverse laborers in all-male communities beyond the influence of women and churches, sailors were often depicted as especially promiscuous and perverse, which is what Melville does on the *Dolly*.

Nonetheless, some readers of *Typee* were shocked, or at least they pretended to be. In the mid-nineteenth century, even literature intended for entertainment was expected to uphold moral standards. Yet just as the Internet has unleashed a flood of pornography, the proliferation of printed materials in Melville's time included erotic literature, while some mainstream writings such as *Typee* pushed the boundaries of respectability. Melville's publishers in Britain and especially America expurgated some of his racier language, though some readers still objected to what one review called *Typee*'s "unblushing walks along the edge of modesty."

As a narrative obsessed with taboos (a Tongan word introduced into English by Cook), *Typee*'s sexual transgressions extend beyond the *Dolly*. Though Tommo adds some less-than-convincing disclaimers, he defends polygamy and depicts the Typee valley as a prelapsarian paradise where sex is free from jealousy and sin. Melville also indulges in sexual innuendo by having Tommo's leg periodically swell, describing fruit with vaginal imagery, and not-so-subtly comparing Kory-Kory's lighting of a fire to masturbation. In queer subtexts that extend to other Melville works, Tommo expresses sexualized affection for Kory-Kory and Toby, and Melville may have known that Polynesian cultures, not unlike whaling ships, were relatively open to homosexual practices. *Typee*'s treatments of sex and sexuality range from the explicit to the euphemistic, the jocular to the serious, and the erotic to the censorious. Modern readers may find instances juvenile, enticing, and surprisingly tolerant, as well as racist and sexist, particularly when the bodies of Indigenous women fall repeatedly under *Typee*'s gaze.

Most important is Tommo's relationship with the olive-skinned, blue-eyed Fayaway, who combines some stereotypical traits of Pacific Island and European women. Fayaway has only a few tattoos, enough to make her exotic without marring her beauty; and she exhibits the sympathy of a Victorian angel in the house while at the same time remaining a "child of nature" free from sexual inhibitions. Unlike the scene on the *Dolly*, however, Tommo's relationship with Fayaway seems caring and mutually fulfilling. The difference may reflect Tommo's growing open-mindedness, though it can also reveal his self-serving hypocrisy and even Melville's own cognitive dissonance, for though Melville elsewhere recognizes the prejudicial power of tropes, he seems less critical when projecting erotic fantasies onto Fayaway, who has little interiority or agency.

This seems especially true during Tommo's escape when he leaves his Typee friends. Fayaway clings desperately to Tommo, but Marheyo has given him a kind of blessing: "He placed his arm upon my shoulder, and emphatically pronounced the only two English words I had taught him—'Home' and 'Mother.'" This moment borders on the bathetic, for Tommo has said nothing of his family or home, and the person he appears to miss most is Toby. Thus, despite its transgressive treatment of sex, *Typee* concludes by invoking the domestic dogma that formed the center of Victorian morality and many a respectable novel of the time. Melville would later upend such orthodoxies in *Pierre*, but the sudden mention of home and family marks the end of Tommo's adventure. For all of *Typee*'s challenging of taboos, cultural values prove deeply ingrained.

Empire

The third controversy of *Typee* begins with Christianity and ends with Western civilization more generally. Though Tommo grants that in theory Christian missions are "a just and holy cause," he emphasizes their pernicious consequences and failures to convert

Native peoples. This angered many reviewers and caused Melville to moderate his comments in a revised edition of *Typee*, but his animus toward missionaries entailed a larger critique not so easily finessed. Pacific Island missions drew on a powerful ideology—the belief that Christianity along with capitalism and white superiority were part of a providential design to spread Western civilization across the globe. One year before *Typee*, the American editor John O'Sullivan coined the term "Manifest Destiny."

Typee disputes such beliefs, depicting Pacific Island missions as participating in a broader degradation of Native life, including the rise of avarice, the abuse of Native laborers, the exploitation of women, and the violence of imperial conquest. Melville was in Honolulu in 1843 when British warships briefly claimed possession of Hawaii, and he was in Tahiti just after France declared the country a protectorate, instigating the Franco-Tahitian War. Tommo denies the moral justification of empire: "Civilization does not engross all the virtues of humanity: she has not even her full share of them. They flourish in greater abundance and attain greater strength among many barbarous people." One outraged reviewer aligned Melville with those who "condemn . . . the gospel of Christ," calling *Typee* an "apotheosis of barbarism." According to such logic, the book was anti-missionary and thus anti-Christian and thus anti–Western civilization.

An important question for *Typee* is the depth and consistency of its critique of imperialism. The book chronicles European abuses and denies white supremacy even as it indulges in primitivist tropes that depict Indigenous people as either bloodthirsty savages or innocent children. Tommo initially subscribes to such dualistic thinking when juxtaposing the supposedly terrifying Typee with the supposedly peaceful Happar, but even after recognizing more complex cultural dynamics, his imagination tends to swing between extremes.

Tommo's escape is particularly complicated. He worries that his hosts want to tattoo or eat him, but some actually want to trade him through a Hawaiian intermediary to an Australian whaler in need of sailors. His exchange on the beach turns chaotic when Typee factions come to blows over whether to let Tommo go. As he escapes in a boat during the fracas, he gives "the only mark of gratitude [he] could show" by tossing bags of gunpowder to a group of women, a musket to Kory-Kory, and a roll of cotton cloth to Fayaway, who is seated on a pile of shingles also brought to trade. Whether seeking a ransom, collecting a finder's fee, or engaging in a kind of gift exchange, the Typee characters are not sequestered in their primitive valley but rather are connected to a global economy built on enforced labor (sailors), violence (guns and powder), resource extraction (shingles), and commodities associated with slavery and industrial exploitation (cotton cloth). For all of Tommo's condemnations of Western conquest, and despite the sentimental parting from his Typee friends, he is a participant in an imperialistic commercial system already gaining foot in the Marquesas.

His role in this system is especially brutal when Mow-Mow, a heavily tattooed warrior who partook in the apparent cannibalistic ritual, swims after Tommo's boat with a "tomahawk" in his teeth. After the pell-mell scene on the beach, Tommo recalls with arresting, time-slowing clarity:

> I felt horror at the act I was about to commit; but it was no time for pity or compunction, and with a true aim, and exerting all my strength, I dashed the boat-hook at [Mow-Mow]. It struck him just below the throat, and forced him downwards. I had no time to repeat my blow, but I saw him rise to the surface in the wake of the boat, and never shall I forget the ferocious expression of his countenance.

Here Tommo commits direct violence against an islander, whom he depicts not as a full human being but as a stereotype saturated with savage tropes. Embodied practices such as cannibalism and—as Samuel Otter has emphasized—tattooing represent the greatest threats to Tommo's cultural identity. When he stabs Mow-Mow, he experiences "horror," the word that Joseph Conrad would use in *Heart of Darkness* (1899) to describe how even well-intentioned opponents of empire succumb to its iniquities.

An issue that remains is whether the ending of *Typee* reveals the limits of Melville's critique or serves as an extension of it. It can be taken to perpetuate conventions of South Sea fiction, indicating a recalcitrant xenophobia that neither Tommo nor Melville can shake. Yet *Typee*'s conclusion may self-consciously expose the ultimate hypocrisy of Tommo, who, despite his supposed cultural pluralism and opposition to empire, has no time for pity or compunction when self-interested push comes to shove. Adjudicating this issue returns to the question: How closely should Melville be identified with his narrator, even if such inquiry risks Tommo's mistake of projecting our own desires and fears onto a situation more interpretable than knowable? Just as Tommo must conjecture about his hosts' motives, readers must speculate about Melville's intentions.

For all the evidence and analysis that one can bring to *Typee*, one purpose of seeking meaning in Melville's work is not to arrive at definitive answers but to face the complexities of the questions that he asks us to ask and that we raise of our own accord. With its wealth of potential subtexts and ironies, *Typee* undermines generic, sexual, religious, and political orthodoxies, though how fundamentally it challenges prevailing beliefs was and remains debatable. That literature is open to interpretation should come as no surprise, but what *Typee* and subsequent Melville texts insist on is that the stakes of interpretation are high—that it is not only an intellectual exercise but a requirement for a moral and meaningful life. Throughout *Typee*, Tommo's life seems to depend on his flawed efforts to interpret a different culture, though by the end of the book an obverse dynamic emerges: it is the Typee people who are most at risk from cross-cultural encounters under empire. Melville only offers hints of how the Typee people interpret Tommo. If he is at least somewhat aware that adventure fiction is complicit in imperial projects, *Typee*'s conclusion and the reception of the novel suggest that such awareness is not in itself enough to transform readers, mitigate systematic wrongs, or exonerate storytellers, howsoever insightful they might be.

A peep at *Omoo* and *Mardi*

It can be tempting to lump Melville's first three novels together. Besides appearing regularly in crossword puzzles, *Typee*, *Omoo*, and *Mardi* are all narrated by young sailors who explore the Pacific Islands while wrestling with existential questions. To varying degrees, all three novels both adopt and ironize the genre of adventure fiction as they pursue thematic interests in empire, cultural pluralism, and sex. *Omoo* and *Mardi* in this sense might be read as extensions of *Typee*, and this chapter's attention to Melville's first novel can model ways for reading his second and third. That said, *Omoo* and *Mardi*, particularly the latter, are distinctive works that indicate Melville's growth as a writer and a thinker.

Omoo is based on Melville's experiences after leaving Nuka Hiva—his participation in a sailors' strike, his subsequent imprisonment, and his wandering around French Polynesia as a laborer and beachcomber. Whereas *Typee* is organized around Tommo's stay in the Typee valley, *Omoo* is a more picaresque novel in which the narrator drifts from adventure to adventure in the company of Doctor Long Ghost, an unscrupulous shipmate on the lookout for food, sex, and liquor. The pair of rovers have no primary goal as they wander a colonial contact zone where they meet a tattooed white man gone native, a Yankee and Brit struggling to start a farm, an abandoned New England–style village decaying in the wilderness, and a series of Native characters who have partially adopted and adapted Western ways.

In what is the closest thing to the climax of the novel, the narrator and doctor gain access to Tahiti's Queen Pomaree. In her chamber, they find "an incongruous assemblage" of Polynesian furnishings and luxurious European goods—a metaphor for the book's cultural heterogeneity that feels less enriching than jumbled. *Omoo* notes the decline of the Tahitian royal family under the pressures of Western imperialism, and the queen herself appears exhausted and unrefined as she summarily dismisses her uninvited visitors. This marks the dispiriting end of the book as the narrator joins another whaling vessel. Despite promises of adventure and attempts at jocularity, *Omoo* is a strangely rudderless narrative reflecting some of the curiosity and more of the disorientation of a cultural borderland. If *Typee* presents a dualistic world in which Indigenous people are beginning to navigate Western contact, *Omoo* depicts a Polynesia already disenchanted by empire.

Mardi dramatizes, among many other things, the impossibility of re-enchantment. The novel begins when the narrator and his buddy leave their whaling ship to explore the Pacific. But if *Mardi* is initially on brand, it soon departs from its predecessors. Reflecting Melville's voracious reading and drive to write what he called in a letter to his publisher "something new" and "original," *Mardi* draws on a dizzying range of sources in history, philosophy, religion, and literature, using the kind of arcane diction and complex syntax that would increasingly define Melville's style. When the narrator murders an island priest while rescuing an idealized young woman named Yillah, *Mardi* takes a fantastical turn unlike anything in Melville's writings. Yillah disappears, and the narrator (now known as Taji) falls in with Media (a king), Mohi (a historian), Babbalanja (a philosopher), and Yoomy (a poet). Together, they seek Yillah through the imagined Mardi archipelago, which becomes an allegory of the world.

Mardi is highly episodic, with 195 short chapters, and what holds the book together is its unceasing exploration—not only Taji's search for Yillah, but also Melville's crossing of artistic and intellectual boundaries. Reviews compared *Mardi* to *Gulliver's Travels* (1726), though Melville even more liberally than Jonathan Swift mixes romantic adventure, political satire, and metaphysical dialogue. Some chapters evoke a mythic, dreamy environment, while others allegorize specific events, including the European revolutions of 1848, the Mexican-American War, and the growing crisis over American slavery. *Mardi*'s strongest continuity with *Typee* and *Omoo* is its sense of lost innocence under imperialism. Stirring adventures at the start of the novel culminate in Taji's discovery of Yillah, but this involves his murder of an Indigenous priest, whose memory and avenging sons haunt Taji, as if *Mardi*'s romance is simultaneously enabled and destroyed by cross-cultural violence.

Melville's contemporaries were generally puzzled and often annoyed by the heterogeneity of *Mardi*, which sold poorly and prompted one reviewer to wonder whether Melville had taken up opium. Modern readers might agree that *Mardi* struggles to find coherent form, though the novel registers an intriguing leap in Melville's artistic vision. The book's intellectual scope, wild style, and sheer bulk make it something of a precursor to *Moby-Dick*—an attempt to break away from the literary conventions that had come to define Melville's work. Prefiguring his later career, the author of *Mardi* resists all constraints. After Taji yet again resumes his search for Yillah, with his avengers close behind, the final line of the novel reads: "And thus, pursuers and pursued flew on, over an endless sea." This sentence, which is hardly a conclusion, points toward a forever questing Melville—the writer that D. H. Lawrence called a "modern Viking" who could not abide the restraints of society, choosing instead to endlessly roam.

Chapter 3
A moving world: *Redburn* and *White-Jacket*

Melville's first three books—*Typee*, *Omoo*, and *Mardi*—focus on exotic adventures. His next two novels, *Redburn* (1849) and *White-Jacket* (1850), also draw on his maritime experiences, but they are more concerned with problems closer to home. Both books describe the development of young narrators who labor under hierarchical systems that simultaneously constitute and constrain their identities. *Redburn* can be read as a Bildungsroman, and *White-Jacket* is something of a reform novel. But just as their protagonists struggle to find their social roles, both books remain uncomfortable with the genres they adopt.

Melville's pivot away from adventure fiction indicates not only his penchant for artistic exploration but also *Mardi*'s poor sales. Needing money to support his growing family, Melville composed *Redburn* and *White-Jacket* in the astonishingly short time of two months each. He described them in letters as commodities—"cakes and ale" written to "buy some tobacco"—though the novels are significantly better than that, as Melville presents his most personal critiques of economic and political inequality, even as such critiques entail skeptical questions about the stability of personhood.

Coming of age

Redburn is crucial to understanding Melville for at least three reasons: it is his most autobiographical book, it is his first coming-of-age novel, and it shifts the center of his social criticism to economic issues. These three aspects of *Redburn* are intertwined insofar as they draw on Melville's poverty-haunted adolescence. He left no letters, journals, or reminiscences from his early years, and, as William H. Gilman has documented, much of *Redburn* is invented or embellished. That said, the novel can be plausibly read as a reflection on Melville's youth. Wellingborough Redburn is the son of a once wealthy merchant who dies bankrupt, leaving the family impoverished, and so Redburn makes his first voyage as a common sailor bound for Liverpool, hoping to follow in the footsteps of his father. Looking back on his privileged childhood, Redburn writes, "[W]hen I think of those days, something rises up in my throat and almost strangles me." Howsoever autobiographical such sentiments are for Melville, Redburn is scarred by emotional loss, dislocation, and choking repression, while his journey offers potential reconciliation and security as he tries to find a place in the world.

Which is to say that *Redburn* is a Bildungsroman. Popularized in the nineteenth century, the Bildungsroman is a coming-of-age novel that follows a protagonist's self-discovery and self-making as they unfold (at least in English-language traditions) within and against larger social structures. The genre typically centers on alienated youths who mature through trial, error, self-knowledge, and self-mastery, even as their intrinsic personalities maintain continuities across temporal change. In this sense, protagonists seem to become the people they have always been, particularly when an older narrator recounts the story of their younger life. Examples from around the time of *Redburn* include Charlotte Brontë's *Jane Eyre* (1847), Charles Dickens's *David Copperfield*

(1850), and Susan Warner's *The Wide, Wide World* (1850)—novels that sold well and focus on characters who lack parental support. That orphans often figure in Bildungsromane can reflect a kind of rootless modernity in which individuals and cultures more generally face the freedom and anxiety of self-making.

Redburn generally follows a Bildungsroman trajectory. We never know the real names of Melville's Pacific Island narrators, as if they are born into new identities when visiting the South Seas. By contrast, "Wellingborough" indicates well-born origins, while "Redburn" suggests the fury of a dispossessed youth. When Redburn leaves home, his older brother gives him a gun and shooting jacket to pawn in New York City—items marking his rural innocence and faded gentility, thus exposing him to exploitation and ridicule. Redburn variously responds with embarrassment, self-pity, and resilience, though most striking is his "misanthropic" rage that at one point impels him to threaten a group of men with his gun. It is hard not to feel bad for Redburn, but he clearly needs to grow up.

And he does. Redburn bears the disdain of his fellow sailors on the *Highlander* before proving his mettle in the rigging, and he learns to check his genteel entitlement as he adjusts to his status as a laborer. Moving beyond self-pity, he sympathizes with Liverpool's poor and desperate Irish emigrants traveling to America. The closest thing that Redburn has to a role model on his journey is the cherished memory of his father, symbolized by the elder's Liverpool guidebook that Redburn carries with him. But when Redburn learns that the city has changed so dramatically as to render the book obsolete, he realizes that "the thing that had guided the father, could not guide the son."

Just as Georg Lukács associates the genre of the novel with "transcendental homelessness," a feeling of being unmoored under capitalist, secular modernity, Redburn finds neither guidance from the past nor role models in the present. The villainous sailor

Jackson, like Redburn at the start of the novel, is a "misanthropic soul" who dies angry. The young aristocrat Harry Bolton squanders his fortune, refuses to accept his reduced station, and remains an incompetent sailor. Harry is not quite Redburn's doppelganger, but he is an uncanny character who shares with Redburn downward mobility and homosocial attraction, the latter implied when the two young men visit something like a gentleman's club in London. The friends ultimately separate, and the novel concludes with the news that Harry has died in a whaling accident, suggesting that Redburn has put Harry's influence to rest, even if Redburn is also working on a whaler at the end of the book.

This final point complicates readings of *Redburn* as a Bildungsroman. Typically, the building of a protagonist's character includes social ascent and familial security; and so as much as the genre celebrates self-making, it often traces conventional paths marked by capitalist gain and heteronormative life. Redburn, however, does not rise through the ranks of a ship or establish himself in a middle-class profession, nor does he marry, establish a home, and start a family of his own. Instead, he ends his story without making much progress, at least as progress tends to be understood.

Redburn's departure from the Bildungsroman genre aligns with a broader economic critique. Gaps between the privileged and poor are everywhere in the novel, and Redburn feels sympathy, horror, and outrage at what he calls "[p]overty, poverty, poverty," most memorably when finding a woman and her children starving in a Liverpool cellar. *Redburn* also resents the callousness and complicity of wealthy characters, though, as with Melville's views of imperialism, the class politics of *Redburn* are complex.

In the mid-nineteenth century, the problem of economic inequality took on particular urgency. As wealth became more concentrated through industrialization, financialization, colonialism, and slavery, the lives of many free laborers were made increasingly precarious by factory production and global trade. In the background of *Redburn* are two specific crises—the prolonged depression that followed the Panic of 1837, and the potato famines of the "Hungry Forties" that devasted Ireland. Melville was also aware of class conflicts raging at various scales, including the European revolutions of 1848 (many of which involved socialist factions), the Chartist movement in England (which *Redburn* mentions), labor unrest in American cities (particularly New York), and work stoppages and mutinies on ships (such as the strike that Melville joined in 1842). As Michael Paul Rogin has shown, Melville's life and writings intersected powerfully with political struggle of his time.

He was, of course, hardly alone in writing about economic disparities. Karl Marx and Friedrich Engels published the *Communist Manifesto* (1848) one year before *Redburn* appeared. Henry Mayhew, in *London Labour and the London Poor* (1851), consolidated earlier articles about the plight of England's lower classes, a subject also treated by novels such as Benjamin Disraeli's *Sybil* (1845) and Elizabeth Gaskell's *Mary Barton* (1848). By conveniently ignoring slavery and the nation's working poor, many Americans of the period saw widespread poverty as a British and European problem. The story of America as a country of independent laborers bound together by sympathy and equal rights remained a foundational narrative, as did the sense that the nation provided an abundance of opportunity to all. Against such views, some American authors wrote about economic inequality—from journalism by George Foster and Margaret Fuller to fiction by Harriet Wilson and George Lippard.

As the story of a young man entering the labor market, Redburn is sensitive to economics. A rich friend of the family gives him a copy of Adam Smith's *Wealth of Nations* (1776), which he tries and fails to read. He also marvels at Liverpool as a hub of global capitalism and valorizes the work of sailors in facilitating international trade.

At the same time, Melville recognizes the uneven distribution of wealth, writing of laborers:

> There are classes of men in the world, who bear the same relation to society at large, that the wheels do to a coach: and are just as indispensable. But however easy and delectable the springs upon which the insiders pleasantly vibrate: however sumptuous the hammer-cloth, and glossy the door-panels; yet, for all this, the wheels must still revolve in dusty, or muddy revolutions. No contrivance, no sagacity can lift *them* out of the mire; for upon something the coach must be bottomed; on something the insiders must roll.

Though Smith warned about excessive concentrations of wealth, he saw free markets as a tide that lifts all boats. By contrast, *Redburn* describes global capitalism as a system built on the exploitation of workers. At the end of Redburn's voyage, Captain Riga contrives to withhold his wages from him.

Melville even goes so far as to compare—and perhaps conflate—capitalism and chattel slavery. Jackson tells stories about the horrors of the Middle Passage, and images of enslaved people adorn furniture, music boxes, and statues on which Redburn dwells. More explicitly, he compares himself to "an African in Alabama" and describes emigrants as "stowed away like bales of cotton, and packed like slaves in a slave-ship." Melville may simply invoke slavery metaphorically to emphasize power disparities, or he may suggest that modern capitalism is not only historically entangled with slavery but also shares with it a ruthless, dehumanizing commodification of workers.

Whatever the case, *Redburn* does not offer any obvious solutions to economic inequality. Charity in the novel comes from good intentions, but alms do little to reduce the general misery. Redburn's visit to the English countryside is pleasantly pastoral but feels like a nostalgic tour of a vanishing way of life. Nor does art offer an escape. The Italian Carlo makes his living by playing the accordion, and his music moves Redburn to wonder whether true value lies in aesthetic pleasure. Carlo, however, strategically adjusts his performances to meet the demands of the market, and so his art is just another commodity, not unlike the printed poems sold by Liverpool beggars. All of which reflect Melville's own resentments as he struggled to make a living from his books.

Organized labor may seem a path toward economic justice in an age of rising worker activism. But if the *Highlander*'s crew bands together to protest the abuses of Captain Riga, their collective action is essentially a prank that does not lead to change. Nor are the sailors a model of solidarity, and the only leader that emerges among them is Jackson, who—like some accounts of President Andrew Jackson—is less a champion of the common people and more a populist bully. *Redburn* further suggests how state power fractures shared class interests when police officers in Liverpool disperse sailors and soldiers who are gathering around a Chartist speaker. Nor does common suffering bring people together, for as Redburn writes of the *Highlander*'s suffering emigrants: "[T]he very hardships to which such beings are subjected, instead of uniting them, only tends, by imbittering their tempers, to set them against each other; and thus they themselves drive the strongest rivet into the chain, by which their social superiors hold them subject."

Redburn himself is not exempt from what Marx described as the alienation of workers from each other. The first chapter of *The Wealth of Nations* discusses the inherent conflict between laborers and employers, but Redburn finds it too dry to finish and ends up using the fly-leaf of Smith's book to work on navigation exercises. This might indicate Melville's disdain for liberal theories of capitalism, or it might signal Redburn's lack of interest in forging solidarity with fellow workers. It can even reveal the educated Redburn's desire to rise above his peers through existing hierarchies insofar as navigation skills could lead to a promotion. But Redburn is never made an officer, even as he becomes a skillful sailor—a trajectory that does not follow the Bildungsroman genre so much as point toward a different ascent.

At least one Marxist reader found *Redburn* inspirational. While being detained on Ellis Island during the height of McCarthyism, the Trinidadian intellectual C. L. R. James wrote *Mariners, Renegades, and Castaways: The Story of Herman Melville and the World We Live In* (1953). James begins the book with a quotation from *Redburn*:

> There is something in the contemplation of the mode in which America has been settled, that, in a noble breast, should forever extinguish the prejudices of national dislikes. Settled by the people of all nations, all nations may claim her for their own.... [O]ur blood is as the flood of the Amazon, made up of a thousand noble currents all pouring into one. We are not a nation, so much as a world.

James finds in *Redburn* a tenuous hope that worker solidarity might someday overcome national and racial divisions to bring forth a more equitable society.

That James was deported for his Marxism is a painful irony, for *Redburn*'s most explicit political statements call not for the organization of labor but for the humane treatment of immigrants. During a rising tide of nativism that would crest with the Know-Nothing Party in the early 1850s, many Protestant Americans who identified as Anglo viewed Irish people as inferior. *Redburn* at times describes Irish emigrants with dehumanizing language, but as Robert S. Levine has emphasized, the book generally defends their interests, as when Redburn insists, "[T]hey have God's right to come." Before the Statue of Liberty and Emma Lazarus's poem welcoming the tired, poor, and huddled masses yearning to breathe free, *Redburn* depicts the United States as a nation with moral responsibilities to immigrants, even if it remains a brutally unequal place.

Ultimately, *Redburn* does not subscribe to optimistic narratives and ideologies. In many Bildungsromane, economic success accompanies self-formation. For Smith, the benefits of free trade are shared by employers and laborers alike. Marx believed that class relations would inevitably lead toward communism. Redburn, however, ends as a common sailor ruminating on the news of Harry's death: "But yet, I, Wellingborough Redburn, chance to survive."

Redburn does not follow a confident arc toward a happily ever after. Redburn may not be on any arc at all in a world seemingly governed by chance. After learning that his father's guidebook provides no guidance, Redburn concludes, "This world, my boy, is a moving world." As Melville's youth may have taught him, no genre, book, or theory can reliably chart a person's course under the uncertainties of capitalism. Perhaps Redburn's acceptance of such conditions is a kind of capitulation. More existentially, it suggests that the universe is without foundations or a designing God that can be known. *Redburn* offers no definitive moral on how to live in a moving world. Perhaps the best one can do is chance to survive and offer fellow-travelers whatever succor one can, even if it is never enough and survivors will always feel haunted.

The disciplined self

After *Redburn*'s critique of economic inequality stops short of specific advocacy, *White-Jacket* turns with similar ambivalence to the related topic of political rights. The book is partly based on Melville's time as a sailor on the USS *United States*, a Naval frigate that he joined in Hawaii and on which he served for fourteen months. *White-Jacket* also draws on Melville's reading in government reports, law books, and naval memoires. The result is a novel with two main narratives: one describes the operations of the *Neversink*, including the abusive treatment of sailors; the other follows the narrator, known only as White-Jacket, whose coat symbolizes an identity that he must leave behind. Working at political and psychological levels, both narratives explore how hierarchies compromise the promise of democratic freedom.

White-Jacket details the structures and protocols that inculcate status differences on the *Neversink*—from surveillance and punishment, to labor and social arrangements, to bodily comportment and modes of address. The finely graded ranks of officers make a chain of command, and though power is distributed less formally among the crew, the men of the foretop and after-guard, at least from White-Jacket's perspective, stand above the lowly waisters and holders. As Max Weber would argue half a century later, modern institutions require hierarchy, specialization, and bureaucratic impersonality. White-Jacket writes of being enmeshed in such systems: "It was enough to make you a man of method for life."

Yet order on the *Neversink* is not absolute. Officers and sailors drink, gamble, steal, and engage in sexual activity, while theatricals, storytelling, and poetry flourish outside of official duties. Individuals assert influence based not on rank, but on competence and charisma. Most dramatically, the *Neversink*'s discipline is not governed by rational management so much as brutal and often arbitrary physical punishment, including flogging—the tying of sailors to wooden frames and whipping their bare backs to the point of unconsciousness. *White-Jacket* condemns flogging by comparing it to slavery and contrasting it with American political principles. Many popular novels of the antebellum period supported social causes such as abolition and temperance, and by joining the anti-flogging movement already underway in America, *White-Jacket* offers itself as a novel of reform. The book even appeals directly to Congress for redress and prompted a review from a rear admiral of the US Navy. At the same time, the book's subtitle—*The World in a Man-of-War*—shows that Melville's concerns go beyond flogging.

A theoretical issue that *White-Jacket* takes up is the tension between ideals of equality, rights, and freedom and the practical need for hierarchy, duty, and control. Echoing the rhetoric of American revolutionaries (such as Melville's grandfathers), as well as that of Jacksonian Democrats (such as Melville's brothers), *White-Jacket* decries the "despotism" and "tyranny" imposed on sailors, who are referred to as "citizens" and "*the people*." As Ralph Ellison wrote of Melville, "Whatever else his works were 'about,' they were also about democracy."

This interest takes specific form in *White-Jacket* when Captain Claret orders the crew to shave their carefully cultivated beards. The mandate nearly sparks a mutiny figured as a political rebellion until threats of flogging and habits of submission convince the sailors to obey. A single holdout is eventually flogged and imprisoned, making him a conscientious objector who (on the one hand) challenges the *Neversink*'s power structure and (on the other) serves a symbolic role that dissipates revolutionary energy. *White-Jacket* typically argues that naval abuses are illegal or that a change in law should render them so. But one year after Henry David Thoreau published "Resistance to Civil Government" (1849), also known as "Civil Disobedience," *White-Jacket's* "Rebellion of the Beards" suggests that natural rights supersede governmental authority. In such instances, the novel is more radical than reformist.

And yet the book remains uncomfortable with absolute equality and freedom. White-Jacket worries that without regulation the crew would become "a mob," a term that political thinkers of the time used to condemn democratic excesses. When Jack Chase, "a stickler for the Rights of Man" and a partisan for Peruvian independence, secures shore leave for the crew in the name of "Liberty!," many of the sailors abuse their freedom so egregiously that White-Jacket observes: "Such are the lamentable effects of suddenly and completely releasing '*the people*' of a man-of-war from arbitrary discipline." These sentiments reflect the conservative views of political theorists like Edmund Burke, as well as those of American Whigs such as Justice Lemuel Shaw, Melville's father-in-law.

For Jennifer Greiman, Melville defends democratic equality while also valuing individual difference. For Larry J. Reynolds, White-Jacket displays an antidemocratic attitude by elevating himself as a foretop man over the lower classes of the *Neversink*. White-Jacket also counts on his racial privilege, thanking God that he is white during the flogging of a Black sailor; and when he himself is unfairly sentenced to be whipped, Chase helps to secure an exception for him as a white and educated member of the foretop.

This does not mean that White-Jacket exhibits a consistent or coherent identity. Bildungsromane bring continuity to personal change, but *White-Jacket* seems skeptical of such self-realization. White-Jacket's presence in the novel waxes and wanes, and the coat by which shipmates and readers know him is an especially unstable trope. The jacket is an improvised hybrid—"bedarned and bequilted" and patched with various "odds and ends." It can signify a piecemeal, shifting identity without foundations or consistency, but it also seems inescapable when White-Jacket fails to sell it at an auction and cannot find paint to change its color. The jacket nearly kills him twice: when the crew mistakes him for a shipmate's ghost and drops a yardarm on which he rests, and when he must cut himself free of the garment to keep from drowning as sailors throw harpoons at him, mistaking him for a great white shark. Even so capacious and fluid a symbol of selfhood threatens to be fatally constraining.

White-Jacket's escape from his coat is a kind of liberation—from his checkered past, from the racial essentialism of whiteness, from the notion that selves can be rendered as legible symbols, and from the domineering structures of the *Neversink* that hail him as White-Jacket in the first place. He marvels at one point,

"[H]abituation to discipline is magical"—and by abandoning his white jacket, he can be taken to leave behind the disciplined selfhood imposed on him. Yet the identity that emerges is not entirely clear, as the novel ends by ruminating on wayward humans wandering an inscrutable world. Here Melville's prose is fancifully extended to the point of self-indulgence, and yet it moves inexorably inward, as cosmic questions become concentrated in the self:

> As a man of war that sails through the sea, so this earth that sails through the air. We mortals are all on board a fast-sailing, never-sinking world-frigate, of which God was the shipwright; and she is but one craft in a Milky-Way fleet, of which God is the Lord High Admiral. The port we sail from is for ever astern. And though far out of sight of land, for ages and ages we continued to sail with sealed orders, and our last destination remains a secret to ourselves and our officers; yet our final haven was predestinated ere we slipped from the stocks at Creation.
>
> Thus sailing with sealed orders, we ourselves are the repositories of the secret packet, whose mysterious contents we long to learn. There are no mysteries out of ourselves.

True enough, in that White-Jacket, after escaping his white jacket, largely disappears from *White-Jacket*, as if his plunge into the sea is not only a kind of slipping from the *Neversink*'s stocks, but also a simultaneous death and rebirth into some new but undefined identity. The habituations of discipline, whether brutal or magical, may violate a person's authentic self, but *White-Jacket* also suggests something harder to grasp—that social structures help to constitute a person, and that leaving them behind, if this is even possible, may mean abandoning one's identity without finding a stable substitute. There may be no self beyond the disciplined self, or at least no knowable self as we travel the ocean-like cosmos.

The endings of both *Redburn* and *White-Jacket* thus strain against the generic and conceptual boundaries of their social critiques. How can the laws of economics or the self-formation of the

Bildungsroman promise security in a chancy, moving world? How can a nation found itself on "We the People," when we can't be sure who persons even are? *Redburn* and *White-Jacket* push social inquiry to the point of philosophical mystery. A fuller sense of the entanglement of the physical and metaphysical culminates in Melville's next book, *Moby-Dick*.

Chapter 4
Four reasons for going to sea in *Moby-Dick*

Where to start with *Moby-Dick*, a book widely considered one of the greatest novels in American and world literature? Authors influenced by *Moby-Dick* are too many to name here but include Nobel laureates William Faulkner, Jean-Paul Sartre, Toni Morrison, J. M. Coetzee, and Olga Tokarczuk. Visual and performance artists such as Frank Stella, Jackson Pollock, Laurie Anderson, and Wu Tsang have based works on *Moby-Dick*, which has a robust presence in popular culture and across a range of media—from graphic novels and children's books, to films in multiple languages, to video games, music by *Led Zeppelin*, and a version made up of two hundred tweets. Whether one prefers *Citizen Kane* or *Star Trek II: The Wrath of Khan*, a coffee at Starbucks or a drink at San Francisco's oldest gay bar, references to *Moby-Dick* are ubiquitous.

But should one start with *Moby-Dick*? The book often serves as an introduction to Melville's writings, despite its length, dense style, intellectual demands, and disorienting amalgam of forms. Many readers who start *Moby-Dick* quit before finishing, particularly when its adventure plot gives way to philosophical speculations and scientific descriptions of whales. It might be better to begin with something else from Melville—the more accessible *Typee*, the generically familiar *Redburn*, or the complex but more manageable short fiction. But one lesson of *Moby-Dick* is that curiosity and ambition, for better and worse, can be hard to abjure.

So how might one start to understand *Moby-Dick*? Biographical context can help to explain the book's extraordinary shape and scope. After writing *Redburn* and *White-Jacket* at high speed, Melville still needed money, and around February of 1850 he began working on a book he called "The Whale." Based on the legendary sperm whale Mocha Dick and the famous sinking of the whaleship *Essex*, the manuscript was mostly done by that summer, until Melville uncharacteristically spent an additional year reworking it. One possible explanation is that he met Nathaniel Hawthorne, whom he praised in a rapturous 1850 review. Melville's letters to Hawthorne during this time—passionate, profound, both whimsical and earnest—reveal an author who knew he was at the height of his powers, even if no one else did. As Melville wrote to Hawthorne in 1851, "Though I wrote the Gospels in this century, I should die in the gutter." This was twenty months after the impoverished Edgar Allan Poe died after being found unconscious on a Baltimore street.

Melville's decision to pursue his highest goals in *Moby-Dick* led to a radically expanded book—the kind of sprawling, heterogeneous, unrestrained novel that Henry James would later call "large loose baggy monsters." Following John Updike, Lawrence Buell places *Moby-Dick* in a tradition of "meganovels" that set a diverse group of characters in a microcosm representing the crises of the age. As an omnivorous book, *Moby-Dick* partakes in multiple genres, including romance, realism, epic, drama, and the novel of ideas. It also ranges across fields of knowledge, especially philosophy, theology, science, history, art, and literature. In doing so, the book metacritically reflects on its status as a meaning-making narrative—and it does all this in a sweeping, sometimes manic style characterized by ornate diction, swelling rhythms, and kinetic alliteration. Monstrous, mega, multigeneric, multidisciplinary, meta, and manic—*Moby-Dick* rewards all manner of reading while eluding any single approach.

Perhaps the best way to begin discussing *Moby-Dick* is to start at the beginning, or more accurately with its first chapter, "Loomings," which does not provide a map of the book but helps to organize possible pathways through it. After Melville's dedication to Hawthorne, after the Sub-Sub Librarian describes his wayward researches, and after an eclectic catalogue of quotes about whales, "Loomings" introduces our narrator, Ishmael, who discusses four reasons why he decided to go to sea, each of which points toward a way to read *Moby-Dick*.

The hypos (psychology)

Ishmael's first reason for going whaling is to find relief from what he calls the "hypos," a general nineteenth-century term for depression, anxiety, and low spirits. Ishmael reveals that he is drawn to funerals, fights, and suicide, and yet he is not an easy narrator to know, for "Call me Ishmael" suggests a chummy informality while still withholding his actual name. As vague as Ishmael's hypos are, they seem related to his isolation. The name refers to the Bible's disinherited Ishmael, of whom an angel decrees, "[H]is hand will be against every man, and every man's hand against him." *Moby-Dick*'s Ishmael is often in his own thoughts, like an "*Isolato* living on a separate continent of his own." He offers no reason for his alienation except for a memory of an abusive stepmother sending him to bed without dinner, where he falls into a reverie and senses a phantom next to him with its "supernatural hand" in his own. Scholars have associated this dream state with maternal abandonment, masturbation, and the uncanny, but whether or not Freud is invoked, Ishmael's isolation seems to have psychological roots. Terrified but unwilling to release the ghostly hand for fear of breaking the spell, the young Ishmael is both threatened by and desperate for human attachment.

The problem of loneliness was hardly new, but it was central to much Romantic literature of the late eighteenth and nineteenth centuries. From Jean-Jacques Rousseau and Johann Wolfgang von Goethe, to William Wordsworth and Mary Shelley, to Ralph Waldo Emerson, Frederick Douglass, and Emily Dickinson, Romantic writers often associated solitude with suffering, creativity, and knowledge. The rise of a Romantic, solitary selfhood accords with the era's liberating but also alienating decline of familial, social, and religious authority. As C. S. Lewis would later write about modern individualism, "The price of freedom is loneliness."

Whether Ishmael can form connections with others is a question at the heart of *Moby-Dick*. As a member of the *Pequod*'s crew, he is part of a lively, diverse community that is nowhere so comforting as when the sailors work together to break up lumps of sperm whale oil. Ishmael writes:

> Squeeze! squeeze! squeeze! All morning long; I squeezed that sperm till I myself almost melted into it; I squeezed that sperm till a strange sort of insanity came over me; and I found myself unwittingly squeezing my co-laborers' hands, mistaking their hands for the gentle globules. Such an abounding, affectionate, friendly, loving feeling did this avocation beget; that at last I was continually squeezing their hands, and looking up into their eyes sentimentally; as much as to say . . . let us all squeeze ourselves into each other; let us squeeze ourselves universally into the very milk and sperm of kindness.

The biblical Ishmael turns his hand against others who turn their hands against him, and *Moby-Dick*'s Ishmael has complicated feelings about the phantom hand from his childhood, but the rhythmic repetitions of the "Squeeze of the Hand" chapter shows our narrator enjoying a deeply satisfying and sensual communion with others.

The most remarkable example of Ishmael's intimacy is his relationship with Queequeg. Though initially horrified by Queequeg's tattoos, tomahawk, and race, Ishmael wakes to find his roommate hugging him "in the most loving and affectionate manner." That Ishmael calls Queequeg's embrace a "bridegroom clasp" suggests that their relationship is sexual, though it is difficult to define precisely. This may be because Melville feared censure at a time in which homosexuality was proscribed and criminalized. It may also be because modern categories of sexuality were in the process of formation, and so specific definitions and labels were less available. Whatever the case, Ishmael quickly accepts Queequeg's racial and cultural differences. Lolling in bed with his "Bosom Friend," the depressed, anxious, isolated Ishmael of "Loomings" becomes "entirely sociable and free and easy."

Whether Ishmael ultimately finds relief from his loneliness is another question. The unity of the *Pequod*'s crew is often based not on mutual affection or understanding, but on Ahab's domineering personality. Ishmael's friendship with Queequeg also slips into the background, and he alone survives the wreck of the *Pequod*, thus losing whatever attachments he had managed to make. Recalling the alienation of "Loomings," the last word of *Moby-Dick* is "orphan."

That said, Ishmael survives the sinking of the *Pequod* by floating on Queequeg's coffin, which is decorated by carvings that match the islander's tattoos, suggesting that their bond and Queequeg's symbolized body remain a kind of lifesaver. When Ishmael is rescued by another whaler seeking its captain's lost son, the full final sentence of *Moby-Dick* reads: "It was the devious-cruising Rachel, that in her retracing search after her missing children, only found another orphan." "[A]nother" implies that the world is full of lonely people (where do they all belong?), but it also suggests that orphanhood is a shared condition and potential basis for affiliation. As Ishmael earlier says of the *Pequod*'s crew, "[F]ederated along one keel, what a set these Isolatoes were!" *Moby-Dick* can be taken to memorialize Ishmael's lost comrades, whose stories he integrates into his own. Even more optimistically, by relating his story to readers, Ishmael invites new attachments. In the Bible, Ishmael is initially disinherited but becomes a father of nations. In *Moby-Dick*, Ishmael alone is saved, and how we judge his psychological and emotional state may finally depend on tone. In contrast to the garrulous, expansive style that dominates most of *Moby-Dick*, Ishmael's language in the "Epilogue" is beautifully restrained: "Buoyed up by that coffin, for almost one whole day and night, I floated on a soft and dirge-like main. The unharming sharks, they glided by as if with padlocks on their mouths; the savage sea-hawks sailed with sheathed beaks." Is this the voice of an exhausted, traumatized survivor, or of someone who has found a kind of peace?

No money (politics)

The second reason that Ishmael goes to sea is that he has "no money," making him another Melville narrator who describes the world from a subordinate point of view. Elaborating on *Redburn* and *White-Jacket*, *Moby-Dick* continues Melville's critique of power as the *Pequod* functions as a political allegory at various levels of scale.

It is, of course, a whaling ship involved in "a butchering sort of business." Hunts are awash with bloodlust and gore, while the rendering of oil in "The Try-Works" chapter turns the *Pequod* into a hellish factory. Authority descends from Ahab, to the middle management mates, to the harpooners and sailors of the forecastle. As C. L. R. James has emphasized, Ishmael's solidarity with the crew is based on the dignity of their labor, but his hiring exposes the oppression of workers when the owners of the *Pequod* compensate him with a pitiful three-hundredth share of whale oil. Mutiny lurks amid such inequality—from discontented sailors, to Starbuck's thoughts of murdering Ahab, to the inset story of the *Town-Ho*. But Ahab maintains his grip on power, not only with the carrot of financial reward and the stick of threatened violence, but also with the magnetic personality that he deploys in "The Quarter-Deck" chapter. Unlike the bureaucratic discipline of *White-Jacket*, Ahab dominates the crew with what Max Weber would term "charismatic authority" as the *Pequod* becomes an exploitive business under Ahab's narcissistic management style.

The *Pequod* can also be read as a ship-of-state representing the United States in crisis. In this context, Ahab is a populist demagogue inflaming the passions of the masses. Melville may have had Andrew Jackson in mind, though ancient Rome, Renaissance Italy, and post-Revolutionary France also reminded nineteenth-century Americans that republics historically devolve into tyranny. By enlisting the crew in the hunt for Moby Dick, Ahab turns his personal grievances into a politics of self-pity and

8. From Thomas Beal's *The Natural History of the Sperm Whale* (1839), a book which Melville consulted when writing *Moby-Dick*.

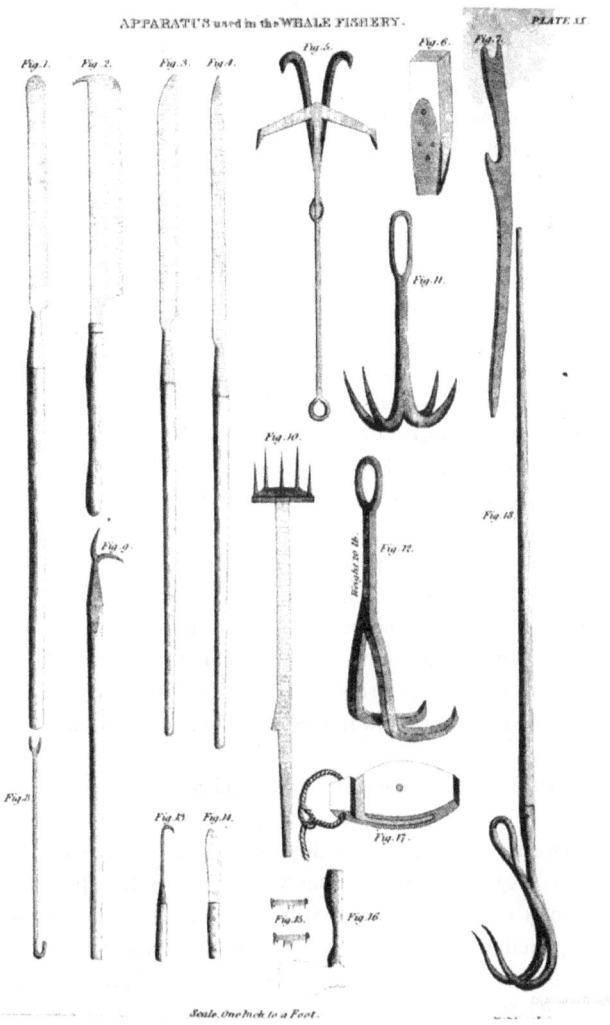

9. Whaling implements as depicted in *An Account of the Arctic Regions* (1820) by William Scoresby, whom Melville quotes in *Moby-Dick*.

vengeance. The disastrous outcome of his regime supports
F. O. Matthiessen's classic view that Melville was committed to
"the possibilities of democracy," and Donald Pease has added that
scholars like Matthiessen canonized *Moby-Dick* during the Cold
War by reading Ishmael as an alternative to Ahabian
authoritarianism.

In a related interpretation, the *Pequod* also invokes the American
slavery crisis. During the composition of *Moby-Dick*, Congress
passed the Compromise of 1850, a set of bills that included a
stronger Fugitive Slave Law that compelled Northerners to return
escapees to their masters. The Compromise sought to ease
sectional tensions but only exacerbated the conflict. Douglass,
who may have crossed paths with Melville in New Bedford in
1839, responded to the Fugitive Slave Law by calling on
Northerners to kill slave catchers and send their bodies to the
South. The law also inspired the century's best-selling novel,
Harriet Beecher Stowe's abolitionist *Uncle Tom's Cabin* (1851–52),
whose first serialized installment appeared four months before the
publication of *Moby-Dick*. More personally for Melville, his
father-in-law, Massachusetts Supreme Court Justice Lemuel
Shaw, upheld the Fugitive Slave Law in the infamous case of
Thomas Sims, whom Shaw returned to slavery in Georgia.

Moby-Dick is generally against slavery and racism, though
Melville's views are not always clear. Queequeg and Pip are
under-realized characters, but they represent a range of virtues.
Ishmael's regard for "divine equality" aligns him with antislavery
principles, and his relationship with Queequeg traces a conversion
from prejudice to pluralistic appreciation. More typologically,
Ishmael from the Bible is the son of the enslaved Hagar, and some
abolitionists used the biblical King Ahab to represent ungodly
slave masters. Yet for all of its egalitarian impulses, *Moby-Dick* at
times depicts Black characters in stereotypical ways, while
Ahab—despite and because of his masterful power—maintains a
kind of appeal. None of Melville's private writings indicate support

for abolitionism, and the antislavery sentiments of *Moby-Dick* and other Melville publications are almost always subtextual, open to interpretation, or complicated by philosophical questions about free will and the nature of evil. When Ishmael asks in "Loomings," "Who aint a slave?," he foregrounds his country's most divisive political issue even as he evades it.

As much as *Moby-Dick* reflects Melville's America, the *Pequod*, like the whaling industry in general, ranges the world with its multinational crew. Whether because of Melville's travels as a sailor, his extensive reading, his doubts about American exceptionalism, or his temperamental resistance to being hemmed in, the *Pequod* can be taken as a microcosm of a borderless world. Celebrating the unbounded freedom of the ocean and invoking an international anarchist, Ishmael refers to the *Pequod*'s crew as an "Anacharsis Clootz deputation from all the isles of the sea, and all the ends of the earth."

Which is not to say that *Moby-Dick* embraces a post-national vision. Ishmael places American whalers above their European competitors, and he chides England for depending on American sperm oil (a section tactfully omitted from the British edition of *Moby-Dick*, along with some homosocial and blasphemous passages, as well as—inexplicably—the epilogue to the book). Though Melville based Queequeg on the Māori chief Te Pehi Kupe, Ishmael reports that the harpooner is born on "Kokovoko," an island "not down in any map; true places never are." The *Pequod* can represent a multitudinous globe, and the ocean for Melville is free from geopolitical constructions, but *Moby-Dick* retains a Western perspective and primarily addresses British and American readers.

This is especially true of the book's depiction of Fedallah, who, as a hodgepodge of Orientalist tropes, is vaguely associated with Persia and Arabia, China and the Philippines, Zoroastrianism and Islam. Melville's culture projected its desires and fears onto an exoticized

East that took on increasing geopolitical significance as European incursions threatened the Ottoman Empire, British penetration into China sparked the Opium Wars, and America's coercive efforts to open Japanese markets led to the Kanagawa Treaty. Wai Chee Dimock and William Spanos have explored parallels between Melville's Romantic individualism and American expansionism, while Edward Said has drawn on historical and modern contexts to take Ahab as a figure of US imperialism.

Ahab's catastrophic quest suggests the hubris of his domineering worldview, while Ishmael offers a different model of international relations—one based not on projecting power but on corrigibility and camaraderie. Here his impoverished status matters, for he does not go to sea as a paying passenger who observes different cultures from a privileged distance. Nor is he a cosmopolitan with the economic and cultural capital to make himself comfortable anywhere in the world. Nor does he consider himself a member of a chosen people, as did the settler-colonist Pilgrims, who defeated the Pequod nation in a genocidal war. Rather, he is a sailor who bunks in the forecastle where he encounters the diversity of the *Pequod*'s crew in a relatively egalitarian way, even as the "Midnight, Forecastle" chapter shows cultural divisions threatening their comity. If Ishmael ends the book as more of an exile than a citizen of the world, *Moby-Dick* largely avoids narrow nationalism with a non-totalizing depiction of global pluralism.

At its farthest spatial limit, *Moby-Dick* complicates the relationship between humans and nature at a planetary scale. Ishmael acknowledges that the whaling industry threatens the extinction of whales, and the book's bloody scenes of hunting can be horrific, especially after "The Grand Armada" chapter depicts whale pods as loving families. With Ahab's rage extending to the solar system itself—"I'd strike the sun if it insulted me"—Melville shows how anthropocentric attitudes toward the environment can be brutally unsustainable.

As an alternative, *Moby-Dick* simultaneously blurs and respects the boundaries between humans and the nonhuman world. Flora, fauna, weather, and the ocean are anthropomorphized in familiar ways, though they also possess strange sentience and agency that Ishmael both admires and fears without fully comprehending. In *Moby-Dick*, human and nonhuman relations are opaque, open-ended, beyond hierarchical ordering, and imbued with various feelings. Whales exemplify this, but so do coral insects, undulating squid, mercurial winds, and the vapor of whale spouts—all of which point to Melville's unsettling ecological imagination and ways to rethink relations between human beings and the environment.

To conclude this section on politics, *Moby-Dick* represents a range of power dynamics, none of which are comprehensive or exclusive. The *Pequod* is an exploitive business headed by an egoistic captain of industry. It is also an American ship-of-state led by a demagogue and doomed by slavery. It is a global microcosm in which an imperial Ahab imposes his will on others. It is part of an ecosystem whose complexity and scope exceed human control and understanding. In all of these readings, Ahab's will to power drives the *Pequod* to destruction, while Ishmael—writing from a subordinate position—offers a more accommodating outlook. This dualistic framework can serve as a starting point for *Moby-Dick*, and yet much turbulence remains.

For all his flaws, Ahab is a multifaceted antihero who elicits the interest and even sympathy of readers, particularly if their obsessions with *Moby-Dick* feel akin to Ahab's monomania. Nor, as Jennifer Fleissner has emphasized, does Ishmael offer an unequivocal alternative to Ahab's tyrannical individualism, particularly when following his captain's lead and pledging to hunt Moby Dick. Indeed, Ishmael and the crew are not simply manipulated by Ahab as they pursue their own desires, form their own relationships, and voice their own points of view. No dualism is absolute in *Moby-Dick*, for as much as the book is about inequality, the powerful and disempowered are not always so easy to differentiate.

This holds true when considering other political topics. Women are almost never mentioned in *Moby-Dick*, indicating a limit of the book, as well as gender biases in canon formation. Yet *Moby-Dick* is insightful when studying gender, especially masculinity, and the book has been a touchstone in gay and queer literary studies for over half a century. On a different front, Melville follows long-standing patterns that conflate physical disabilities with moral depravity, though Ahab has nuanced views of his injury as an embodied and philosophical condition. As these lines of inquiry suggest, *Moby-Dick* can anticipate, or at least converse with, a wide range of modern political questions. From the American Civil War, to the Cold War and ongoing struggles for civil rights, to wars over oil and the instabilities of Western empire, to climate change and the rise of ethno-national populism, readers have found, and will no doubt continue to find, that *Moby-Dick* speaks to the world in which we live.

Water (philosophy)

The third reason that Ishmael goes to sea is hard for him to explain but somehow involves water. He notes in "Loomings" that the streets of Manhattan lead "waterward," that city shores are lined with "water-gazers," that people subconsciously wander toward water, that artists are often enchanted by water, and that "meditation and water are wedded forever." Ishmael ends his reverie by citing Narcissus, who drowned trying to embrace his reflection in a fountain: "[T]hat same image, we ourselves see in all rivers and oceans. It is the image of the ungraspable phantom of life; and this is the key to it all." Here, "this" refers most directly to our reflection in water, as if self-knowledge is the slippery secret to truth. But "this" might also refer to Ishmael's claim that the "image" of "the phantom of life" is "ungraspable," and that the key to knowledge begins in knowing that what we see may not be real and that some truths remain beyond reach. Uncertainty about the attainability of truth—call it skepticism—surfaces throughout *Moby-Dick*.

Like the Sub-Sub-Librarian (who gleans his reading from "the long Vaticans and street-stalls of the earth"), and like Ishmael (for whom "a whale-ship was my Yale College and my Harvard"), Melville was an autodidact who picked up philosophy from treatises, encyclopedias, popular articles, and conversations over drinks. He was hardly a system builder, and his philosophizing is both serious and playful, as suggested by Eleanor Melville's memory of her grandfather allowing her to build book houses with his collected works of Arthur Schopenhauer. *Moby-Dick*'s philosophical references can be dizzying, often intentionally so, though Melville returns to a set of skeptical challenges that are concentrated in the white whale, whose unknowability does not signal an absence of meaning so much as an excess of possibilities.

One way to get at the truth of whales is through empirical science. *Moby-Dick*'s "Cetology" chapter cites natural philosophers on whales while using observation and classification to define them systematically. However, such efforts fail to capture the marvelous variety of whales; and when Ishmael invents a taxonomy based on sizes of books, the result is more whimsical than scientific. Other morphological approaches to whales in *Moby-Dick*—chapters that dissect and describe their bodies, the measuring of a whale skeleton—tend to begin with objective rigor before veering into conjecture and satire. This is not to say that Melville rejects science or sets it in opposition to literature. What he resists are empirical projects that would reduce the power and beauty of nature to disarticulated material facts—a charge that some nineteenth-century Romantics directed not only at scientists but at empirical philosophers such as John Locke and David Hume. When Ishmael ends his would-be taxonomy of whales ("God keep me from ever completing anything"), *Moby-Dick* implies that scientific systems can never be comprehensive.

Another way to think about reality in general, and the white whale in particular, is to look beyond the material world. When Starbuck insists that Moby Dick is only a "dumb brute" with no special or hidden significance, Ahab responds:

> All visible objects, man, are but as pasteboard masks. But in each event—in the living act, the undoubted deed—there, some unknown but still reasoning thing puts forth the mouldings of its features from behind the unreasoning mask. If man will strike, strike through the mask! How can the prisoner reach outside except by thrusting through the wall? To me, the white whale is that wall, shoved near to me.

Ahab can be associated with philosophical idealism—a tradition stretching from Plato, to Rene Descartes and Baruch Spinoza, to Immanuel Kant and Samuel Taylor Coleridge. *Moby-Dick* names all these thinkers, who generally believed that the material world is a secondary expression of a more fundamental reality—that what we experience through our physical perceptions are shadows, images, phenomena, or illusions. Ahab denies that the white whale is just a white whale, and his hunt is a quest for deeper truths that Moby Dick symbolizes and, in doing so, conceals. Ahab aspires to strike through the mask of materialism, though he acknowledges, "Sometimes I think there's naught beyond."

Ishmael also dabbles in philosophical idealism, though his comportment differs from Ahab's. In the "The Mast-Head" chapter, Ishmael describes a "young Platonist" who ascends the rigging to look for whales but becomes lost in "unconscious reverie":

> [A]t last he loses his identity; takes the mystic ocean at his feet for the visible image of that deep, blue, bottomless soul, pervading

> mankind and nature; and every strange, half-seen, gliding, beautiful thing that eludes him; every dimly-discovered, uprising fin of some undiscernible form, seems to him the embodiment of those elusive thoughts that only people the soul by continually flitting through it. In this enchanted mood, thy spirit ebbs away to whence it came; becomes diffused through time and space.

In this passage, the idealist penetrates physical surfaces to dimly discern elusive truths that hint at a oneness of self and nature. Whereas Ahab seeks to violently possess the hidden meanings that bedevil him, "The Mast-Head" imagines a different sort of revelation—the melting of identity into a universal order marked not by anger and antagonism, but by enchantment and harmony.

Such idealism is not entirely comforting. At the end of "The Mast-Head," Ishmael warns young Platonists about releasing their grip on the material world, and—not unlike Narcissus or White-Jacket—losing their selves by plunging into the sea. Most ominously, "The Whiteness of the Whale" chapter describes how white is not only a color registered by the senses but also the signifier of a godless, nihilistic universe that stirs horror in the soul. Similarly, when Pip is abandoned in the ocean and witnesses the foundations of reality, the experience so radically reshapes his consciousness that the crew considers him insane.

Melville's ambivalence about both materialism and idealism points to a larger dynamic insofar as *Moby-Dick* does not advocate for a specific philosophy, but rather is committed to juxtaposing the disparate epistemologies with which different characters make meaning. Famously, "The Doubloon" chapter depicts various characters interpreting a coin that Ahab has nailed to the mast. Ahab the narcissist sees only himself as idealism slides into solipsism. The Quaker Starbuck sees only signs of God's righteousness, though his optimism seems overdetermined. The materialist Flask sees only an economic token he can use to buy cigars. Queequeg, at least according to Stubb, sees only the button from a king's trousers, suggesting both innocence and inventiveness. The mysterious Fedallah "only makes a sign to the sign," indicating the unending possibilities of interpretation. By the time Pip responds to the doubloon by chanting, "I look, you look, he looks; we look, ye look, they look," the only thing clear is that a multitude of perspectives render a multitude of potential meanings—none definitive and together suggesting that foundational truths are ungraspable or do not exist. Readers attempting to interpret Moby Dick or *Moby-Dick* face a similar challenge. Or, as Ishmael says of the sperm whale's brow, "Read it if you can."

None of which means that *Moby-Dick* is skeptical or relativistic to a point where all views are equally valid, virtuous, or wise. Pip registers a powerful subjectivist claim, but leaves us in kaleidoscopic confusion. At the other extreme, Ahab's monomaniacal search for truth, as dramatically and philosophically compelling as it might be, remains fatally self-centered and absolutist. Though Ahab briefly reconsiders his quest in "The Symphony" chapter, his ending—tied to a symbol of unattainable truth by his own harpoon and rope—suggests that it may be better to accept the limitations of human knowledge. Ishmael models such philosophical modesty, for as much as he shares the interpretive drive of idealists such as Ahab, he learns—or is forced—to be less insistent when he ends *Moby-Dick* floating on the surface of the sea instead of drowning in its depths. Recognizing that the phantom of life is ungraspable may not be the key to it all, but Ishmael escapes the doom of Ahab and Narcissus by letting fundamental truths lie.

Providence (religion)

The final reason that Ishmael gives for going to sea is not about his own motivation. After invoking "Providence" and "the Fates," he doubts in "Loomings" if he chose to go whaling in the first place:

I think I can see a little into the springs and motives which being cunningly presented to me under various disguises, induced me to set about performing the part I did, besides cajoling me into the delusion that it was a choice resulting from my own unbiased freewill and discriminating judgment.

In addressing the conundrum of free will versus determinism, *Moby-Dick* draws on long-standing intellectual traditions—from classical notions of fate, to mechanistic accounts of the universe, to Christian ideas of an omnipotent God who providentially orders all events.

In some ways, *Moby-Dick* leaves no place for free will. Ishmael invokes the Fates of classical mythology, and the book resembles a Greek tragedy when Ahab proclaims as he finally faces the white whale and fulfills the prophecies of the book, "This whole act's immutably decreed." In a different register, the *Pequod*'s cycloid pots and Ishmael's references to "Descartian vortices" suggest that the world is physically and metaphysically governed by ineluctable mathematical laws. As if inhabiting a clockwork universe, characters in *Moby-Dick* are sometimes described as mechanical—even the willful Ahab, who thunders, "The path to my fixed purpose is laid with iron rails, whereon my soul is grooved to run."

Most frequently, *Moby-Dick* discusses determinism within a Christian framework. The Dutch Calvinism of Melville's mother, as well as the Puritan influence on early American literature, exposed Melville to concepts of God's sovereignty that denied or severely curtailed human agency. Focusing on Job's efforts to escape God's will, Father Mapple, in "The Sermon" chapter, preaches submission, but the "grand, ungodly, god-like" Ahab follows other heaven-defying protagonists—Goethe's Faust, Byron's Manfred, and Mary Shelley's Victor Frankenstein. At the root of such figures is Milton's Satan, to whom Ahab is repeatedly compared. In Book 10 of *Paradise Lost* (1667), God confidently explains to the angels that Adam was destined to sin and that God foresaw his fall, but that Adam would nonetheless be punished for a choice that to many modern readers seems hardly a choice at all. In his copy of *Paradise Lost*, Melville scribbled next to this section, "All Milton's strength and rhetoric suffice not to satisfy, concerning this matter—free-will."

Neither does *Moby-Dick* provide a satisfying answer, if only because Melville is not trying, like Milton, to justify the ways of God to man. It is never clear whether the white whale is a dumb brute, an intelligent actor, an agent of God's providence, or some kind of god itself. We do not know whether Ahab is destined to hunt Moby Dick or simply invokes fate to vindicate his choices. Nor is it easy to draw a moral from Ahab's end without knowing the extent of his agency. Ishmael is not sure if he chooses to go whaling. Queequeg believes that people decide when they will die. And Melville further complicates the issue in "The Mat-Maker" chapter by adding chance to free will and fate as potential causal forces. As with *Moby-Dick*'s juxtaposition of materialism and idealism, Melville is less interested in taking a position on providence than in exploring how to live with its unresolvable possibilities.

Yet again, Ahab can stand as a cautionary example. He lacks what John Keats took to be a characteristic of great artists—the "*Negative Capability*" of "being in uncertainties" without feeling irritation or anger. More religiously, Ahab furiously asks why God's providence required him to lose his leg. It is a problem of theodicy: How can a benevolent, all-powerful God allow his creations to suffer? Ahab does not or cannot accept the explanation that God works in mysterious ways, and he directs his hostility at Moby Dick: "He piled upon the whale's white hump the sum of all the general rage and hate felt by his whole race from Adam down."

An important question is how much of Ahab's blasphemy should be attributed to Melville himself. From Tommo's tolerance of

Polynesian beliefs to Ishmael's respect for Queequeg's pagan faith, Melville's writings express a religious pluralism unusual for his culture. Combine this with his critiques of Christianity and his conflicts with the Protestant press, and Ahab's quarrel with God can be taken to voice Melville's own religious unbelief. Yet *Moby-Dick* also implies that Ahab's transgressions deserve the punishment they receive and that Ishmael, an unconventional but not ungodly man, is wiser not to resent providence.

Michael Colacurcio has argued that to question God seriously requires one to be open to the possibilities of faith. Melville wrote to Hawthorne just after finishing *Moby-Dick*: "I have written a wicked book, and feel spotless as the lamb." Perhaps Ahab provided Melville some release, allowing him to relinquish, if only momentarily, his skeptical charges against Christianity, the most enduring of which involved how humans should regard an inscrutable and seemingly unjust providence. Perhaps Melville also found in Ishmael a more sustainable approach to addressing religious uncertainty—one that eschews Ahab's rage and, without having much of a choice, accepts that God is beyond human knowledge.

How to end a discussion of *Moby-Dick*? The best answer is probably that you don't. *Moby-Dick* revels in unanswerable questions about intimacy, justice, truth, and agency—all of which are portended by Ishmael's opening musings about his reasons for going to sea. In similar fashion, a phrase from the epilogue of *Moby-Dick* can stand as a kind of conclusion. After Ahab is yanked from his whaleboat, after Moby Dick attacks the *Pequod*, and after the ship and its crew sink into the Pacific leaving nothing but a whirlpool behind, Ishmael—who has seemingly disappeared from the story—resurfaces to find himself "floating on the margin" of the whirlpool's diminishing vortex.

Ishmael is indeed a marginalized character, not only as a narrator displaced by Ahab, but also as an isolated laborer with no money and little power. Saved by Queequeg's coffin, he survives the wreck of the *Pequod*—not by striking through masks and discovering deep truths (too dangerous and ungraspable), nor by willing himself to heroic action (which may not even be possible in a deterministic world), but rather by drifting on the suddenly peaceful sea and waiting to be rescued. Unlike Ahab, Ishmael survives, making it possible to extract some advice from *Moby-Dick*. Newton Arvin found in the end of the book a call for "cosmic submissiveness"—for accepting the limits of one's knowledge and living with, instead of trying to dominate, nature. There may be some wisdom or necessity in floating on the surface of experience, though what happens to Melville in the wake of *Moby-Dick* aligns him more with Ahab than Ishmael.

Chapter 5
Antagonisms: *Pierre*, *Israel Potter*, and *The Confidence-Man*

Imagine that you've written the best book of your life, suffered mentally during its composition, sacrificed financial security and familial harmony in the process, and sent your opus into the world only to be met with mixed reviews and disappointing sales. *Moby-Dick* was not ignored or consistently panned, as legend sometimes has it, but what praise the book received from Melville's contemporaries was decidedly outweighed by their confusion, ambivalence, and charges of impiety. To judge by Melville's next three novels—*Pierre* (1852), *Israel Potter* (1855), and *The Confidence-Man* (1857)—he reacted to the reception of *Moby-Dick* with despair and bitter bemusement, though he also felt to some extent liberated from the public that he had failed to please. Melville's style and thematic interests remain recognizable, often developing along established trajectories. But after *Moby-Dick*, he largely abandons sea novels, as if leaving behind—or like *White-Jacket*, cutting himself free from—the authorial persona he had crafted. Melville's fictions after 1851 become more sardonic and involuted, while his innovations, driven as always by curiosity and ambition, feel newly motivated by animus.

Big feelings

There are many reasons to love and hate *Pierre*, though Melville's contemporaries focused almost exclusively on the latter. One review called the novel an "incoherent hodge podge" of "inconceivable and incongruous propinquity," while the title of another simply pronounced: "Herman Melville Crazy." Reviewers did not just excoriate *Pierre*; some recommended that people stop reading Melville altogether. He was not cancelled, but almost a year after its publication, *Pierre* had sold only 283 copies. One of the ironies of the book's reception, and of Melville's midcareer more generally, is that the transgressions that outraged nineteenth-century readers are partly what make *Pierre* so fascinating today.

To appreciate *Pierre* fully is to recognize that the novel is simultaneously ironic and deadly serious. On the surface, the story starts pleasantly enough. The scion Pierre and angelic Lucy enjoy their engagement in bucolic upstate New York. Perhaps Pierre is overly familiar with his mother and a bit too sensual in general. Perhaps readers notice that his wealth depends on an exploitive manor system in which farmers rented from aristocratic families who, in the case of Pierre's ancestors, killed Indigenous people and held slaves. Perhaps, too, Melville's initial prose is so mellifluous as to arouse suspicion: "There are some strange summer mornings in the country, when he who is but a sojourner from the city shall early walk forth into the fields, and be wonder-smitten with the trance-like aspect of the green and golden world." Notice this sentence's accessible diction, smooth rhythm, and balanced consonance. It is as if Melville is hoping to appease the public with a newly domesticated and dulcet style.

He is not. Pierre finds circumstantial evidence that the darkly beautiful, friendless Isabel is the illegitimate child of his dead father. Impelled by Christian charity and family loyalty—and, it must be admitted, a barely repressed libido—Pierre puts Isabel under his protection by pretending to marry her. What could possibly go wrong? After his mother disowns him, Pierre moves to the city to pursue a writing career where he lives in poverty with Isabel, Delly (a fallen farm girl), and Lucy (who improbably follows him). The relationship between Isabel and Pierre remains ambiguous, but they ardently feel and may act upon passions that (at best) are unsanctioned by marriage and (at worst) are incestuous. As foreshadowed by allusions to *Romeo and Juliet* (1597) and *Hamlet* (1603), *Pierre* ends in murder and suicide. But unlike Shakespeare—or another touchstone for the novel, Dante—Melville refuses to assert a moral order. *Pierre* entices readers with the promise of romance only to violate their most sacrosanct beliefs.

Even gesturing toward the possibility of incest was taboo in the nineteenth century. When Harriet Beecher Stowe publicly condemned Lord Byron's liaison with his half-sister, she herself was condemned for broaching the subject—and this was Stowe, a paragon of Victorian virtue, not the suspect author of the unchaste *Typee* and impious *Moby-Dick*. And there's more. In addition to Pierre living with three unchaperoned young women, one of whom may be his half-sister, his potential sexual offenses include flirtations with his mother and a "love-friendship" with his male cousin Glen. Melville's culture was not the first or last to worry about family values, but it did witness the Mormon practice of plural marriage, the Oneida community (which coined the term "free love"), and a rising women's rights movement that challenged marriage norms. Romantic writers of the period, many referenced in *Pierre*, were known to take lovers outside of marriage—not only men such as Byron, Goethe, and Percy Bysshe Shelley, but also Madame de Stael, Mary Shelley, Margaret Fuller, and George Sand. It was not the sexual revolution of the 1960s, but pockets of rebels reimagined sex and marriage while incurring predictable censure.

More fundamental than the erotic transgressions of *Pierre* is the book's challenge to moral standards more generally. Pierre's mother appeals to virtue but is most concerned with appearances. The Reverend Falsgrave is an unctuous hypocrite. Pierre is not some villainous libertine easily judged and comfortably punished, but rather a naïve, earnest idealist who values (howsoever partially, self-servingly, and annoyingly) righteousness and truth. Yet Pierre cannot be sure of his duty, for when weighing the evidence of Isabel's parenthood, he struggles to move from inference to certainty. In his confusion, he comes across a pamphlet by the transcendental philosopher Plotinus Plinlimmon, who asserts that we live in a fallen world in which we can never know God's laws and thus are always susceptible to error.

Not unlike Captain Ahab, the problem with Pierre is that he dogmatically follows his "irresistible intuitions" without regard to his fallibility, and that such intuitions remain inseparable from his passionate urges and delusions of grandeur. Pierre assures Isabel that their attachment is like the love between angels, but he is drawn to her "wantonly as it were, and yet quite ignorantly and unintendingly." Four years before the birth of Sigmund Freud, *Pierre* depicts human psychology as driven by repressed sexuality. The scandalous possibility broached by *Pierre* is that moral laws are unknowable and that humans are so driven by unconscious, base desire that they only appear to deliberate, decide, and act. It is thus hard to blame Pierre for his apparent choices. When the novel tells its readers, "Judge ye, then, ye Judicious," it decidedly feels like a threat.

If eroding moral foundations was not enough to make Melville's contemporaries hate *Pierre*, the novel practically invites a backlash by attacking the enterprise of literature itself. Melville mocks the shallow taste and narrow piety of reviewers who heap undeserved praise on Pierre's juvenilia, while he derogates publishers more interested in marketing and profit than shepherding quality work. The only successful writer in *Pierre* is Charlie Millthorpe, an entrepreneurial hack, and many of Melville's complaints appear in a chapter titled "Young America in Literature," a slap at the influential circle of New York literati with whom Melville had associated.

Pierre also parodies domestic fiction, a wildly popular genre that often involves courtship plots in which heroines struggle to square their feelings with societal expectations. By learning to discipline their unruly hearts, and thereby teaching readers to do the same, protagonists of domestic novels were typically rewarded with marriage and motherhood. The genre was often written and read by women, while representing—and sometimes challenging—ideals of femininity based on home life, Christianity, sexual virtue, and self-sacrifice. Hawthorne fumed in 1855, "America is now wholly given over to a d—d mob of scribbling women, and I should have no chance of success while the public taste is occupied with their trash." Such comments show how domestic fiction threatened male authors who felt entitled to rule the marketplace.

Pierre's plummet from blissful engagement to unmarried misery reverses the trajectory of domestic novels, as does Pierre's spectacular failure to regulate his emotions. By choosing the tempting Isabel over the fair Lucy, *Pierre* further departs from generic expectations, and Melville's opening chapters lampoon the sentimental style of some domestic fiction. It is hard to take seriously sentences such as this: "Love is both Creator's and Saviour's gospel to mankind; a volume bound in rose-leaves, clasped with violets, and by the beaks of humming-birds printed with peach-juice on the leaves of lilies." *Pierre* also includes a narrative voice that acknowledges the story's status as fiction, admitting that the style of *Pierre* is "irregular" and reluctantly agreeing to sketch Lucy's history only because readers expect it. That the young Pierre was an avid consumer of novels seems to indict its popular forms as he moves beyond the moralistic "novel-lessons" that the narrator describes as "false."

And yet Melville, for all his satiric edge, acknowledges the corrective force of such lessons. A moral available in *Pierre* is not so different from that of much domestic fiction: one should not uncritically indulge one's feelings, but rather corrigibly and honestly modulate them within complicated social contexts. Pierre, however, rejects communal and interpersonal influence. He immediately recoils when Lucy asks him to share his secrets with her, and many of his disastrous decisions are made in solitude. For all his sexual and mystical affinities with Isabel, the final line of dialogue in *Pierre* is her cry: "All's o'er, and ye know him not!" If domestic fiction is about the emotional labor of managing one's interiority in relation to the interiority of others, Pierre remains profoundly self-centered. Perhaps he should have attended to some novel lessons after all.

Pierre's problematic egoism is only compounded by his uncompromising attitude toward art. Though the manuscript scraps on which he labors are difficult to evaluate, their grandiose pessimism can sound as absurd as *Pierre*'s earlier sentimental effusions. Romanticism valorized the agonistic, typically male genius suffering for extraordinary art, but nothing indicates that Pierre's writing is actually any good. Indeed, the style of *Pierre* itself appears both serious and self-parodying:

> Pierre was solitary as at the Pole. And the great woe of it all was this: that all these things were unsuspected without, and undivulgible from within; the very daggers that stabbed him were joked at by Imbecility, Ignorance, Blockheadedness, Self-Complacency, and the universal Blearedness and Besottedness around him. Now he began to feel that in him, the thews of a Titan were forestallingly cut by the scissors of Fate. He felt as a moose, hamstrung. All things that think, or move, or lie still, seemed as created to mock and torment him.

One might love or hate such grandiose style. One might simultaneously love *and* hate it. The concatenating phrases, heaped and flushed with superlative, archaic, and colloquial diction, echo the audacious language of *Moby-Dick*. But in *Pierre* such writing feels particularly ironic when amplifying the protagonist's egoism.

At such moments, the novel might be retitled *A Portrait of the Artist as a Self-Regarding, Insufferable Young Man.*

This seems especially true when Lucy and Isabel, artists in their own right, offer to assist the struggling Pierre by adding their own "original writing" to his. Pierre reflexively rejects collaboration: "Impossible! I fight a duel in which all seconds are forbid." Given the tragic outcome of *Pierre*, Melville seems as critical of male-coded Romanticism as he does of female-coded domestic fiction. We need not go as far as Nancy Fredericks's claim that *Pierre* exemplifies "Melville's feminism," but the book does concede what domestic novels elaborate: self-reliance looks foolish and destructive when passions run unchecked.

Nor does *Pierre* exempt Melville from this charge. Like Melville, Pierre descends from a Revolutionary War hero, enjoys some early celebrity as a writer, falls from gentility into financial distress, and has a father who may have had an illegitimate daughter. Pierre's failure to publish a truly great work can point to Melville's uncertainties about his own books, as well as the painful sacrifices he made (and imposed on his family) when writing them. When the narrator of *Pierre* proclaims, "I write precisely as I please," it sounds like the boast of a liberated author, but seeing how disastrously this attitude serves Pierre can give a reader pause. Perhaps Melville after *Moby-Dick* was working through not only outwardly directed antagonisms, but also some guilt and self-doubt. He certainly despaired of ever fulfilling his grandest artistic visions; or, as *Pierre* proclaims, "[A]ll the great books in the world are but the mutilated shadowings-forth of invisible and eternally unembodied images in the soul." *Pierre* is an ambitious, iconoclastic novel about the costs of ambition and iconoclasm. Melville recognized and paid many of the costs, as if when he was writing *Pierre* he was unable or unwilling to heed the warnings of his book. In Branka Arsić's words, "Melville's literature will always be about its own failure."

Big lies

Melville's next novel, *Israel Potter*, tells the story of a soldier, sailor, and spy who participates in key moments of the American Revolutionary War but is neither rewarded nor remembered. There are legitimate reasons why *Israel Potter* is almost as forgotten as its protagonist. Much of its prose lacks the expansiveness of Melville's later style, and the plot wanders as Israel's life unfolds with little agency or dramatic logic. Israel himself is inconsistently portrayed as access to his thoughts and feelings fluctuates. And yet these flaws have meaning, as if Melville's design is to perform a kind of failure.

The uncharacteristically subdued prose of *Israel Potter* refuses to idealize the American Revolution. As the leaders who fought for independence from Britain passed from life into hagiography, antebellum America memorialized their accomplishments—from the Washington Monument (begun in 1848), to histories by George Bancroft, Jared Sparks, and William Cooper, to historical novels by Lydia Maria Child, James Fenimore Cooper, and William Gilmore Simms. While some writings reflected the complexities of the Revolution, many offered up uncritical patriotism. In "What to the Slave is the Fourth of July?" (1852), Frederick Douglass complained to his listeners that unthinking "zeal" was a "staple of your national poetry and eloquence."

By contrast, Melville punctures American myth-making in his depictions of Benjamin Franklin (a maxim-spouting hypocrite), John Paul Jones (a smooth-tongued narcissist), and Ethan Allen (a bombastic bully). The language of these Revolutionary heroes is manipulative and grandiloquent, and when *Israel Potter* elevates its style when describing the battle between the *Serapis* and *Bon Homme Richard*, Melville suggests that extravagant language obscures the brutal realities of war.

Israel Potter also doubts that the American Revolution was guided by the hand of God. In Israel's half-a-century of wandering, random incidents shape his life, so much that Melville writes, "[A]ll human affairs are subject to organic disorder; since they are created in, and sustained by, a sort of half-disciplined chaos." Unlike the Founding Fathers, Israel gets no praise when he returns to America in 1826. Instead, he is almost run over by a Fourth of July parade on the fiftieth-year anniversary of "The Declaration of Independence," the very day on which both John Adams and Thomas Jefferson died in what was seen as a providential concurrence. Israel's name suggests God's favor, but as much as Americans claimed the story of *Exodus* for themselves—and as often as *Israel Potter* alludes to Old Testament lions, deserts, and bricks without straw—the novel makes it hard to take the United States as God's chosen country.

It is tempting to read *Israel Potter* as a tribute to a common man who embodies the ideals of American democracy better than the Founding Fathers. Yet Israel is not a stable national type. He is born in Connecticut, identifies as American, and exhibits a natural independence, but he also traps in Canada, hunts whales off the coast of Africa, sails through the Pacific Islands, works in France, and spends most of his life in England, where he raises a family without becoming a citizen. As Rodrigo Lazo has emphasized, Israel is something of a transnational migrant. A pirated 1865 version of the novel was titled *The Refugee*, and Israel is frequently described as an "exile" and a "fugitive." This later term can link his story to the genre of fugitive slave narratives, particularly when he is described as "subject to enslavement" when fleeing impressment and imprisonment.

But if Ishmael wonders, "Who ain't a slave?" *Israel Potter* asks, "[W]ho ain't a nobody?" In this sense, the vagaries of Israel's character—naïve and ironic, active and passive—destabilize his identity. He also impersonates a dead squire, dresses as a scarecrow, serves as a spy, and reinvents himself as Peter Perkins aboard a British warship. If *Israel Potter* ultimately fails to vividly portray its protagonist, this can indicate Melville's doubts about the consistency and transparency of selves. When Israel dies as a stranger in his homeland, we might think of Isabel's last line in *Pierre*, "All's o'er, and ye know him not!" We can also look forward to Melville's next book, which challenges the very notion of character.

The big con

The Confidence-Man is Melville's last novel, if it can be considered a novel at all. The story takes place on a Mississippi steamboat that is only vaguely described, and its plot describes a series of episodes in which potential swindlers accost an assortment of passengers, none of whom are portrayed in depth. A single con man or the Devil may be adopting personae, but the book never confirms or denies such possibilities. With its indistinct setting, flat characters, disjointed narrative, and unresolved dramatic and moral questions, *The Confidence-Man* is far from a conventional novel, but it remains a brilliant experiment and the foremost example of what Nina Baym has called "Melville's Quarrel with Fiction."

Melville was dedicated to the art of the novel, but he always pushed the limits of its form. *Typee* plays with the tropes of adventure romance, *Mardi* is as much an allegory as a novel, *Redburn* is not quite a Bildungsroman, *Moby-Dick* is a glorious mashup of genres, and *Pierre* parodies domestic fiction. More than any of Melville's books, *The Confidence-Man* is a metafictional work that flaunts its artificiality. Samuel Taylor Coleridge wrote in 1817 that imaginative literature should evoke in its audience the "willing suspension of disbelief," but *The Confidence-Man* encourages its readers to disbelieve almost everything—from perception and reason, to the foundations of identity, to the purposes of literature itself.

The impossibility of distinguishing truth from falsehood is immediately apparent in the book. *The Confidence-Man* is subtitled "His Masquerade," and its action takes place on April Fool's Day aboard a steamer named the *Fidéle*, which comes from the Latin word for *trust*. In chapter 1, three signs on the deck of the boat further foreground the problem of belief—a placard warns of a "mysterious imposter," a chalkboard held by a seemingly deaf and mute stranger extols the virtues of "Charity," and a sign outside the barbershop reads, "No trust," that is, no credit accepted. Subsequent chapters sketch a range of possible scams as characters ask strangers to trust them, often by relating parable-like stories that may or may not be true. The word "confidence" and its derivatives appear 207 times in the book, along with "trust" (154), "belief" (50), and "faith" (21), while the frequencies of "seem" (196), "look" (170), and "appear" (69) suggest the difficulty of parsing truth and fiction.

A cluster of nineteenth-century cultural contexts justify suspicion in *The Confidence-Man*. Rising urbanization and geographic mobility put Americans in increasing contact with strangers, exposing them to various schemes that were reported in the popular press. Other phenomena smudged the boundaries between appearance and reality—from racial and ethnic passing, to P. T. Barnum exhibits and fake news, to the spread of advertising and cosmetics. New belief systems such as spiritualism, Fourierism, and transcendentalism found followers but were often regarded as humbug, as were pseudoscientific claims about phrenology and animal magnetism. The development of global capitalism also brought uncertainties as consumers did not know who produced their goods, merchants relied on far-flung networks, speculative bubbles inflated and popped, and the financialization of the economy depended on a shared but tenuous confidence in abstract representations of value. As a New Yorker who grew up during a financial panic, launched his writing career by mixing fiction and fact, was once impersonated by a con man, and had an uncle who was caught embezzling, Melville had personal experience with the manipulation and fragility of social trust.

The problem of belief is also central to philosophical skepticism. *The Confidence-Man* draws from a host of thinkers who focus on our susceptibility to deception, including Plato (references to caves and shadows abound in the novel), classical skeptics (such as Diogenese Laertius), Descartes (who begins his *Meditations* with the section "Concerning Those Things That Can Be Called into Doubt"), Michel de Montaigne (see his essay "That It Is Madness to Judge the True and the False"), and David Hume (who wrote about the unreliability of the senses and inductive logic). All of these philosophers dwell on the fallibility of belief, though the thinker that *The Confidence-Man* most directly engages is Ralph Waldo Emerson.

Melville read Emerson, attended one of his lectures, and had mixed feelings about America's leading transcendentalist. "I do not oscillate in Emerson's rainbow," Melville wrote to Hawthorne in 1851, but "I love all men who *dive*." In *Moby-Dick* and *Pierre*, Ahab and Plotinus Plinlimmon reflect aspects of Emerson's thought, but *The Confidence-Man* explicitly represents him in the character Mark Winsome (while Winsome's disciple Egbert stands in for Henry David Thoreau). Winsome claims that beauty, love, and truth always accompany each other, an optimism that he extends in theory to rattlesnakes but not in practice to fellow humans. When Winsome refuses to aid a beggar (based on Poe), Emersonian philosophy seems both socially corrosive and logically incoherent, even as Winsome blithely proclaims, "I seldom care to be consistent," thus echoing Emerson's famous line from "Self-Reliance" (1841), "[A] foolish consistency is the hobgoblin of little minds."

The Confidence-Man does not disagree, particularly in its most metafictional chapters that quarrel with readerly expectations. Chapter 14, "Worth the Consideration of Those to Whom It May

Prove Worth Consideration," describes how a merchant and fellow traveler agree to trust in the goodness of humankind. The twist is that after ordering champagne, the merchant suddenly renounces his confidence, an example of what the narrative calls "the queer, unaccountable caprices of his natural heart." This introduces Melville's complaint that readers want characters to be stable—that for them, "there is nothing a writer of fiction should more carefully see to . . . than that, in the depiction of any character, its consistency should be preserved." As if using Emerson's philosophy to preempt hostile reviews, chapter 14 makes the case that people in "real life" are inconsistent.

Two subsequent chapters extend this line of inquiry. Chapter 33 denies the expectation that novels should represent actual life by claiming instead that great fiction reveals "more reality, than real life itself can show." Chapter 44 elaborates this argument without offering a history of aesthetics or theory of mimesis, though both chapters express the Romantic view that art should not reflect objective reality like a mirror so much as manifest subjective visions that illuminate deeper truths about the world. Whether *The Confidence-Man* rises to this standard is a tricky question, especially if one doubts that its metafictional chapters should be taken seriously at all, for—like the book's potential swindlers—their arguments are circuitous to the point of irony and obfuscation. Even when *The Confidence-Man* steps outside its artificial story, distinguishing truth from falsehood remains a dubious business, as if fiction itself is a kind of con.

Such skepticism may leave readers wondering about the purposes of *The Confidence-Man*. Like a mystery novel or detective story that ends without resolution, the book concludes with the noncommittal line, "Something further may follow of this Masquerade." The point may be that we never arrive at truth—that rational inquiry is really just rhetorical manipulation, that nothing indemnifies us from deception, that any suspension of disbelief must be willfully blind, and that the very nature of trust presupposes a lack of certitude. Emerson celebrates the inconsistency of selfhood and the need to accept an ever-unfolding and perhaps illusory world, but *The Confidence-Man* seems more interested in teasing the reader by enforcing the limits of knowledge.

The book can feel like an intricate puzzle that plays an existential joke on its audience, and we might find its masquerade impressively constructed, intellectually stimulating, and helpfully attuned to the dangers of both deception and dogmatism. But *The Confidence-Man* becomes more than a thought experiment if its dramatization of the problem of belief has stakes that, for all Melville's irony, feel real. Can a reader sympathize with the disabled Black beggar who sleeps on paving stones warmed by the sun as he plays on and suffers from racism? We might feel superior to greedy or self-righteous characters who succumb to potential schemes, but might we also feel tenderly toward "a clean, comely, old man, his head snowy as the marble," who trusts in the Bible, cares for lost children, and buys some dubious medicine for the cough that is killing him? We can read "The Metaphysics of Indian-Hating" chapters as a commentary on the mystery of iniquity, but we might also, like Leslie Marmon Silko, find a critique of US policies toward Indigenous peoples—a critique that insists on the importance of integrity, which is a kind of consistency.

All this is to say that *The Confidence-Man* need not be taken as an entirely ironic text. By occupying a microcosm in which isolated individuals pursue self-interest without regard to truth or the welfare of others, a reader might ask if they want to live in such a world—imaginatively or in reality. If so, *The Confidence-Man* presses the limits, not only of belief, but of skepticism. It suggests that caring for others and searching earnestly for truth, though always risky and prone to error, brings meaning to experience. For William James, the problem of doubt impels us to commit to values and beliefs. "I can believe," he wrote, "that worse things than being duped may happen to a man in this world."

Chapter 6
Melville's magazine fiction

Melville's turn to short fiction in the early 1850s was not exactly a choice. *Pierre* so severely damaged his reputation that publishers were reluctant to invest in another novel, and in 1853 Melville failed to find a buyer for a manuscript that has since been lost. Magazines often published short stories anonymously, allowing Melville to distance himself from his tarnished brand. They also paid by the page, a fast and predictable form of compensation that was not contingent on sales and that the cash-strapped Melville may have preferred. Between 1853 and 1856, Melville published five stories with *Putnam's Monthly* that he later collected in *The Piazza Tales* (1856), and he placed an additional nine pieces in *Harper's Monthly*, another new outlet in the booming magazine industry.

Melville's short fiction is an excellent entry point to his work, allowing readers to attend to the challenges of his thought without being overwhelmed by the scope of his novels. Though his tales tend to be less centrifugal in style, they often share the richly allusive texture and subversive irony of his books. They also dwell on subjects that had long fascinated Melville—from social inequality and the role of art to faith, science, free will, and human nature. Some stories are more like sketches with concentrated themes, while others offer intricately constructed narratives with multifaceted ambiguities. Four Melville tales aptly represent the latter: "Bartleby, the Scrivener" (1853), "Benito Cereno" (1855), "The Encantadas" (1854), and "The Paradise of Bachelors and Tartarus of Maids" (1855).

"Bartleby, the Scrivener"

One way to approach "Bartleby, the Scrivener" is to ask what is wrong with the guy. He initially appears to be merely odd—passive, emotionless, and extraordinarily diligent as a copyist for the lawyer who narrates the tale. Then Bartleby stops working, refuses to leave the office, and rejects all efforts to help or cajole him with the famous phrase, "I would prefer not to." Some commentators have diagnosed Bartleby as depressed, autistic, or anorexic, though dominant interpretations of the story tend to be guided by less physiological explanations.

The story is subtitled "A Story of Wall-Street," and Bartleby can be seen as a victim of capitalism. In the mid-nineteenth century, Charles Dickens, Elizabeth Gaskell, and Rebecca Harding Davis wrote fictions about the plight of laborers in the wake of the Industrial Revolution. "Bartleby" differs in that it focuses on a poorly compensated clerk in a bureaucratized information economy, though the story also challenges hard distinctions between manual and office work. The narrator brags that he was a lawyer for John Jacob Astor, one of the wealthiest men of Melville's time, and he proudly reports that he does "a snug business among rich men's bonds and mortgages and title-deeds." Bartleby's productivity is valuable to the lawyer, who, despite expressions of sympathy and gestures of charity, runs a dehumanizing office. Bartleby's coworkers are called only Turkey, Nippers, and Ginger Nut, and their routinized work is detached from social meaning. Like Karl Marx, who was a foreign correspondent for the *New York Tribune* in the 1850s, "Bartleby" depicts class relations in which the bourgeoisie profit from reified workers who are alienated from their products, each other, and their own selves. When Bartleby stops copying, he is fired, evicted, and imprisoned where he eventually dies of hunger, thereby exposing the coercion at the heart of the lawyer's business and the broader economic system.

Some readers view Bartleby not only as a victim of capitalism, but also as a kind of conscientious objector, so much so that after the mismanagement of mortgages, title-deeds, and bonds caused the financial crisis of 2008, protestors in the Occupy Wall Street movement circulated copies of "Bartleby." That Bartleby's "passive resistance" so effectively flummoxes the lawyer may vindicate Henry David Thoreau's "Resistance to Civil Government" (1849), an essay based on the night he spent in prison for opposing the Mexican-American War and that later influenced the nonviolent resistance of Mahatma Gandhi, Martin Luther King Jr., and Cesar Chavez. Bartleby's death has even been read as a kind of hunger strike against capitalism and consumerism. When he says in the prison yard to the visiting narrator, "I know you . . . and I want nothing to say to you," he can be taken to condemn the lawyer's complicity in and disavowal of economic exploitation.

In a related interpretation, Bartleby's labor resembles that of a disenchanted writer. The lawyer twice contrasts the paperwork of his office with poetry, while the story associates writing with monotonous copying, bodily pain, and dead-end jobs. Melville knew the mental and physical costs of his vocation, and he felt financially pressured to duplicate his early adventure novels rather than pursue more original work. "Bartleby" can thus figure Melville's frustration in that the scrivener is a poorly paid author who refuses to copy, stops writing, earns nothing, and eventually starves. When the lawyer reports that Bartleby once worked at the Dead Letter Office where correspondence without recipients goes, we might think of Melville's ongoing struggle to find sympathetic readers for his work.

At the same time, important elements of "Bartleby" are reducible to an economic critique. Bartleby makes no demands on his boss and forms no alliances with his officemates. Unlike labor organizers in Melville's America, nothing in the story appeals to the rights and dignity of workers or envisions an alternative structuring of society. Perhaps Bartleby has already been broken by the system, and the tale's intention is not to offer solutions so much as dramatize the need for change. Still, one might doubt if better working conditions would ultimately make a difference for Bartleby, who is so inaccessible and seemingly damaged as to raise more existential questions.

As the lawyer mulls over the mystery of Bartleby, he consults Jonathan Edwards and Joseph Priestly on the question of free will. Both philosophers denied that humans have free volition, suggesting that Bartleby may not lack political power so much as metaphysical agency. Edwards in particular defined free will as the capacity of an individual to execute preferences—to choose one thing over another—and so when Bartleby repeats, "I would prefer not to," he may be asserting his agency (I would prefer to do something other than make copies), or he may indicate that he lacks any capacity for preferences (which is to say that he lacks free will). Interpretation becomes even knottier when we ask how realistic Bartleby is supposed to be. Is he a character whose exaggerated but essentially truthful example suggests that humans do not have agency, or is he an absurd thought experiment that shows how ridiculous it is to imagine a person without preferences? To ask such questions is to think less about economic justice and more about human nature.

Which seems exactly what the narrator prefers to do as he simultaneously participates in and agonizes over Bartleby's plight. He initially profits from his scrivener and certainly takes his authority over his employees for granted. But after Bartleby ceases to work, the lawyer allows him to stay in the office, gives him money, and even offers to take him into his home. In his unfolding interactions with Bartleby, the narrator seems driven by greed, guilt, loneliness, conflict avoidance, and public appearances, but he also responds with care and sympathy, even as his charitable instincts bring him a "delicious self-approval." At times, the lawyer distances himself from Bartleby's situation by calling him "the victim of innate and incurable disorder." At other times, he feels a "fraternal melancholy" for a man who, like the lawyer, has no life outside of the office. "Bartleby" may portray a modern condition in which people—bosses and employees alike—are alienated by their dehumanizing work. Or perhaps, as Melville often suggests in his writings, isolation is an unavoidable aspect of life.

"Bartleby, the Scrivener" has inspired a range of interpretations, many of them mutually exclusive, not only from scholars of American literature, but also from theorists and philosophers such as Jacques Derrida, Gilles Deleuze, Jacques Ranciere, and Giorgio Agamben, all of whom focus on Bartleby's indeterminacy. The narrator's final cry, "Ah Bartleby! Ah humanity!" can be taken as genuine mourning for the scrivener and the inescapable heartbreak of life, or it might be a hypocritical denial of responsibility and feckless retreat into sentiment. For Dan McCall, "Bartleby, the Scrivener" is most centrally about the lawyer, whose example compels us to ask how we interpret Melville's story, how we understand our responsibilities to others, and how our own motives and judgments might not be as different from the narrator's as we might like to think.

"Benito Cereno"

"Benito Cereno" is Melville's most explicit engagement with slavery, and his most cunningly constructed text, giving readers some sense of what the story is about but little clarity on what it might mean. The narrative follows Amasa Delano, Massachusetts captain of the *Bachelor's Delight*, who meets a distressed slave ship in isolated waters off the coast of Chile. If you haven't yet read "Benito Cereno," you should do so now, for it is something of a mystery story whose ending can be spoiled.

Though based on actual events as reported in an 1817 travel narrative, "Benito Cereno" is elaborately imagined. The tale is saturated with gothic tropes and historical references, and it is written from a limited third-person perspective whose inconsistency makes it difficult to distinguish objective facts from Delano's subjective experience. Delano suspects that something is amiss aboard the *San Dominick*, seemingly captained by the Spaniard Benito Cereno, but he struggles to discern that the ship is actually controlled by African rebels led by the Senegalese mastermind Babo. Delano repeatedly misreads clues, including a series of knots, locks, and tableaus that simultaneously invite and obscure interpretation. In retrospect, Delano is one of the most obtuse characters in American literature.

Part of the problem is that his sunny view of human nature indicates a profound lack of understanding. Yet Delano is not merely stupid or naïve, nor simply a racist who cannot conceive that Black people have intelligence and agency. Nor is he only a hypocritical, self-styled republican who laments that slavery makes men abusive even as he offers to purchase Babo and hopes to profit by salvaging the *San Dominick*'s human cargo. In addition to all of these evident flaws, Delano willfully maintains his ignorance, repressing the uncomfortable thoughts and feelings that everywhere intrude on his tranquility. It takes undeniable proof—Babo attempting to stab Cereno—for Delano to realize that a rebellion has occurred.

Yet even this moment, described as a "revelation," does not actually disabuse Delano, as confusion reigns even at the level of syntax: "Not Captain Delano, but Don Benito, the black, in leaping into the boat, had intended to stab." This is one of the best worst sentences in all of literature. The revelation promises clarity but itself must be untangled, for "Benito Cereno" is a mystery story whose apparent resolution brings as many questions as answers. The depositions that follow the climactic retaking of the *San Dominick* purport to serve as a "key" to the story but only represent the voices of white people, just as Babo's refusal to speak before his execution precludes any closure to the tale. After witnessing, repressing, and then participating in the violence aboard the *San Dominick*, the unshakably optimistic Delano asks Cereno, "[Y]ou are saved; what has cast such a shadow upon you?" Cereno only answers "The Negro," thus ending all conversation as he goes to a silent death. The Spaniard's final line might invoke the terror of Babo, the general horrors of enslavement, the natural depravity of humankind, or his own guilt-ridden psyche. Whatever the case, what is most clear is that Delano remains willfully ignorant, as if Melville anticipates a point that James Baldwin would make a century later about denials of American racism: "It is the innocence which constitutes the crime."

Melville's critique is not nearly as forthright as Baldwin's, but it works in a similar vein. Delano's obtuseness can point toward Melville's contemporaries who increasingly preferred a Christianity that de-emphasized sin, celebrated America's Manifest Destiny, saw history as a process of constant improvement, and refused to register the evils of slavery and racism. With Delano hailing from Massachusetts and Cereno exhibiting the stereotypical traits of a Southern plantation owner, "Benito Cereno" can be read as an allegory of the United States in which an ignorant Northerner laments the cruelty of slavery but ultimately chooses racial solidarity and economic self-interest when supporting a master who appears to be in charge but is actually paralyzed by the violence of slavery. Or considering that the ship is named the *San Dominick* and its events are set in 1799, the story—as Eric Sundquist has argued—conjures the revolution in Haiti (formerly known as Santo Domingo), the most successful slave rebellion in the Atlantic world and a terrifying example for slaveholders. Considering its allusions to Christopher Columbus and the "Black Legend" of Spanish conquest, "Benito Cereno" relates its events to broader histories of colonialism across the hemisphere. Even further, the text's allusions to political revolutions in Britain, France, and Italy imply that no social system is safe from cycles of oppression and rebellion.

In fact, "Benito Cereno" offers so many historical coordinates that readers might find themselves confounded, placing them uneasily in the position of Delano, who witnesses "foreshadowing," "significant symbols," and "secret sign[s]," but fails to interpret them correctly. The tricky narrative perspective of "Benito Cereno" opens an ironic gap between Delano and Melville, but it also encourages readers to experience the story through Delano's problematic point of view. No evidence suggests that Melville's contemporaries took "Benito Cereno" to be about racist ignorance or cognitive dissonance more generally, but readers today may find that the story—not unlike "Bartleby, the Scrivener"—asks them to critically examine their capacities for judgment and moral action in the face of suffering and injustice, particularly if they follow Delano's lead and are slow to recognize what is happening aboard the *San Dominick*.

"Benito Cereno" thus analyzes and even warns against self-perpetuating beliefs in slavery and racism, though it should be noted that the rebels, howsoever justified, follow their ex-enslavers in acts of extreme violence, only some of which may be necessary. With atrocities occurring on both sides of the color line, "Benito Cereno" remains difficult to locate politically. Babo's silence at the end of the story can support numerous and not always compatible claims—that Melville is not interested in the interiority of Black people, that he is sensitive to the dangers of white authors attempting to represent such interiority, that he is dramatizing the fact that African Americans were silenced by a repressive culture, that (in Gayatri Spivak's view) the very structures of narrative make it hard for subordinate people to speak and be heard, and that Babo continues to act heroically by finding power in silence. Or it may be, as Sterling Stuckey has argued, that "Benito Cereno" represents aspects of nineteenth-century Black culture as Melville understood it through his exposure to African-influenced music, dress, and dance.

"Benito Cereno" reveals the cruelty and hypocrisy of slavery, even as it avoids direct statements on the issue. Like many Americans before the Civil War, Melville disapproved of chattel bondage but apparently saw no way to end it without a devasting conflict, so much so that he sometimes views slavery as a problem that only the future can solve. By inverting the relationship of masters and enslaved people, "Benito Cereno" also suggests that Melville saw no escape from human error and no way to abolish abuses of power—that, as his sense of history tends to show, someone's foot is always on someone's throat. Perhaps "Benito Cereno" can be best understood as antislavery but not abolitionist, a position that recognizes the wrongness of chattel bondage but lacks the conviction for advocacy or activism. Modern readers might feel disappointed in Melville while also acknowledging that the right side of history is easier to judge in retrospect and that "Benito Cereno"—despite and because of its ambivalence—offers lessons that remain relevant today.

"The Encantadas"

Melville's later fiction is bleak, but it never reaches a point of nihilism, even when imagining a fallen world in which humans find no place and scant hope. "The Encantadas" comprises ten sketches of the Galapagos Islands written from the perspective of a narrator who, like Melville, once visited the region aboard a whaling ship. The series is not a connected narrative, but it forms a rough chronological trajectory: early sketches describe the primordial geography and animals of the islands, while later pieces introduce sailors, castaways, and settlers, as well as geopolitical contexts. Life in "The Encantadas" remains a struggle stretched across an immense time frame as Melville shows humans leaving only traces on a landscape that seems indifferent to their fate.

The protagonist at the start of "The Encantadas" might be taken to be the environment itself. Dominated by volcanic cinders, wiry brush, and parched ground, the islands project "desolation," "blankness," and "emphatic uninhabitableness." Biblical and mythic allusions associate the setting with a hellscape abandoned by God or the gods, yet the islands are so starkly depicted that it takes an effort to read them metaphorically. Under relentless physical description, cinders feel most like cinders.

Yet the environment of "The Encantadas" is not self-explanatory, for Melville was writing during a paradigm shift in conceptions of natural history. The model of an unchanging, clockwork universe designed by a benevolent God for the benefit of humans came under stress from scientific developments demonstrating that the Earth was much older than implied by the Bible, that climate and habitat change organisms, that humans are part of (not above) the animal order, and that species and even the solar system itself are subject to extinction. Jean Baptiste Lamarck and Charles Lyell were among early scientists who paved the way for Darwin's theory of natural selection, which he based on his research in the Galapagos Islands in 1835, six years before Melville's own visit. Darwin would not publish *On the Origin of Species* (1859) until after "The Encantadas," but Melville's sketches draw on Darwin's published journals and present a view of natural history that emphasizes the fight for survival across long periods of time. Like Darwin, Melville in "The Encantadas" does not dispute Christian faith, but God seems largely absent from the islands.

As Michael Jonik has emphasized, humans also appear to lack special dispensation. The anthropomorphizing of birds and dogs blurs boundaries between people and animals, as does the atavism of some island dwellers, most notably the "beast-like" Oberlus. The tortoises of "The Encantadas" further destabilize distinctions between humans and nonhumans. At times, they are commodities harvested for oil and sold to ships as food. At other times, they bear metaphysical meanings signifying death or Hindu cosmology.

Most powerfully, they are agential natural beings strangely connected to humans. The narrator recalls lying in his hammock listening to tortoises bump against objects on deck, and he seems to admire and even sympathize with them. That night he dreams of tortoises—"[W]ith them I lost myself in volcanic mazes; brushed away endless boughs of rotting thickets"—but his surprising identification proves fleeting when he happily dines on tortoise meat the next day. As subjects sharing a harsh environment with humans, the tortoises of "The Encantadas" seem both inscrutably alien and deserving of respect. As such, they resemble the whales of *Moby-Dick*, though Melville's ecological imagination in "The Encantadas" is more restrained when speculating about relations between species. Rather than occasioning wild proliferations of interpretation, Melville's tortoises demand a kind of epistemological austerity reflecting the landscape itself.

In some ways, the feeling of "The Encantadas" shifts when sketches introduce humans and the settlement of the islands. The seventh sketch, "Charles' Isle and the Dog-King," traces the rise and fall of a colony and the failures of imperialism more generally. Having helped Peru secure its independence from Spain, a Cuban Creole is granted control of Charles' Isle, but after he declares independence from Peru and becomes a tyrant backed by an army of dogs, his subjects in turn declare independence from him, and the colony descends into a "*Riotocracy*." The Dog-King, who is based on two historical figures, reflects broader geopolitics of the Global South—the decline of the Spanish Empire, revolutions across Latin America, and the instability of republics and dictatorships alike. Melville seems equally fearful of autocracy and mob rule, though as Cristopher Freeburg has argued, "The Encantadas" consistently challenges imperialist narratives of progress. Not unlike the misanthrope Oberlus, who establishes slavery on Hood's Isle in the ninth sketch, the Dog-King shows how colonial dreams give way to violence and chaos before fading away.

A possible alternative to the sketches of the Dog-King and Oberlus is the story of Hunilla, "The Chola Widow." Her stranding on Norfolk Isle, the deaths of her husband and brother, her likely sexual assault by whalers, and the necessity of her abandoning some beloved dogs all make her story a tragic one that calls forth the sympathies of the narrator. That she is a mixed-race Indigenous woman can sharpen the sense of her struggle and resilience when the narrator proclaims, "Humanity, thou strong thing, I worship thee, not in the laurelled victor, but in this vanquished one." The longest sketch in "The Encantadas," and the only one that takes a sentimental tone, Hunilla's story offers some hope for redemption in a largely but not entirely hostile world.

And yet like "Bartleby, the Scrivener," which also includes a narrator's appeal to "Humanity," the moral architecture of "Norfolk Isle and the Chola Widow" is destabilized by problems of sympathy. The narrator expresses pity for Hunilla, and he and his shipmates take up a collection for her. But he also congratulates himself when displaying his generous feelings and takes a kind of aesthetic pleasure in witnessing and relating Hunilla's plight. The narrator wishes that he could draw her in crayon, "tracing softly melancholy lines." He imagines the drowning of her husband and brother as if it were a picturesque painting. Without Hunilla's knowledge, he follows her to her husband's grave and describes her lying prostrate upon it, writing of his motives, "It was not curiosity alone, but, it seems to me, something different mingled with it." What this something is remains unclear. It could be real sympathy, a desire to spy, or an effort to sensationalize her story. Indeed, when the narrator conspicuously refuses to mention Hunilla's sexual assault, and in doing so draws attention to it, he purports to respect her privacy even as he exposes the tragedies of her life. The sketch can thus criticize not only the narrator, but also readers who enjoy pitying victimized people and artists who pander to such desires.

Though "The Encantadas" is not a unified narrative, its final sketch brings together the natural and human histories of the islands. Titled "Runaways, Castaways, Solitaries, Grave-stones, etc.," it presents the Galapagos as a refuge for people suffering political oppression. Yet Melville has shown how tyrannies reconstitute themselves, and so the only escape in "The Encantadas" seems to be solitude or death, represented by the sketch's abandoned huts, unread messages in bottles, and grave markers. These tokens reflect the failed projects of the Dog-King, Oberlus, and Hunilla, and they recall how Melville begins his series by detailing the inhospitableness of the environment.

For all the dreams and nightmares of human settlement, the islands remain largely unchanged, as if the narrator is a kind of archaeologist studying the remnants of a lost civilization. Nature ultimately outlasts any human endeavor—a feeling echoed in other works of the period, such as "Ozymandias" (1818) by Percy Shelley, *The Last Man* (1826) by Mary Shelley, and *The Course of Empire* (1833–36) by Thomas Cole (whose paintings Melville viewed in New York City). The opening sketch of "The Encantadas" claims that the "special curse" of the islands is that "change never comes." By contrast, the "signs of vanishing humanity" with which the series ends might cause twenty-first-century readers to think about parched earth, brutalizing heat, the extinction of species, and how the relationship between humans and nature can involve too much change. Be that as it may, "The Encantadas" imagines a world in which humans are history.

"The Paradise of Bachelors and the Tartarus of Maids"

Melville wrote three tales that are sometimes called "diptychs"—stories that by juxtaposing pairs of sketches invite readers to compare them. The most intriguing of these is "The Paradise of Bachelors and the Tartarus of Maids," which discusses the economic and gendered dynamics of reproduction. In the first half of the story, the narrator joins a group of London lawyers, whom he compares to "Templars," the often-mythologized order of medieval knights known for an asceticism and celibacy that ultimately gave way to corruption. True to form, Melville's lawyers eat and drink with gusto, and what the story describes as their "degenerate" fraternizing is homosocial to the point of queerness.

The bachelor was a recognizable figure in nineteenth-century literature, featured in popular works such as Washington Irving's *Sketchbook* (1820), Charles Dickens' *Pickwick Papers* (1837), and Donald Grant Mitchell's *Reveries of a Bachelor* (1850). "The Paradise of Bachelors" draws directly on Irving's book and follows the conventions of bachelor fiction, presenting the lawyers as sentimental men who eschew both the competition of the marketplace and the comforts of heteronormative family life. The bachelors may not be gay in a modern sense, but they evade traditional masculine roles as they relish their male companionship.

More specifically, by living without heterosexual commitments, they are free from the problem of overpopulation. At the beginning of the nineteenth century, the political economist Thomas Malthus warned that because births increase more rapidly than food production, the seeming expansion of civilization inevitably leads to starvation. Such concerns appeared in various debates over the Corn Laws in Britain, the Great Famine in Ireland, and poverty around the globe. In "The Paradise of Bachelors," other men worry about "the rise of bread and fall of babies," but the lawyers have "no wives or children to give an anxious thought." With their evening of pleasure-seeking consumption associated with "moral blight," "The Paradise of Bachelors" can be seen as an escape from or denial of starker realities.

Problems of reproduction are more glaring when the narrator visits "The Tartarus of Maids," a paper factory based in part on a trip that Melville made to a Massachusetts papermill. The sketch details a distressing scene in which young women labor listlessly in an industrial system that makes them into mechanical slaves. Their dehumanizing work implicates the lawyers from the first half of the diptych, for the mill makes its paper from rags sourced in London and the foreman is a devilish man named Old Bach. Just as the twenty-first century's digital revolution depends on poorly compensated workers, the nineteenth-century's information economy was no paradise for scriveners, factory girls, or struggling authors like Melville.

Moving from industrial production to sexual reproduction, "The Tartarus of Maids" uses gynecological imagery to conflate the labor of manufacturing with the labor of birth. To get to the mill, the narrator travels along "Blood River" through "Black Notch" and a pass called "the Mad Maid's Bellows'-pipe." In the mill's "blood-like, abdominal heat," the paper begins in a vat of "white pulp," runs through a machine with "erected swords," and is cut with a sound "as of some cord being snapped." The entire process takes nine minutes and leaves the female workers exhausted. Writers from Katherine Phillips to Anne Bradstreet to Mary Shelley compared the writing of literature to childbirth, but the women in "The Tartarus of Maids" are virgins who produce only blank paper, suggesting that their labor is not analogous to birth so much as a sterile replacement of it.

"Old maids" were an increasing feature of antebellum New England life, as economic downturns impelled men to seek their fortunes elsewhere, leaving many young women to join an industrializing economy, including jobs at the innovative Lowell Mill. Commentators often praised the Lowell system for providing its female workers with vocational and educational opportunities in a strict moral setting. But if some women appreciated such benefits, they found few prospects for marriage at a time when the spinster became a literary type who, like the figure of the bachelor, did not conform to traditional gender roles.

Like *Typee*, *Moby-Dick*, and *Pierre*, "The Tartarus of Maids" shows Melville's enduring ambivalence about the sexual mores of his time. That the narrator is a "seedman" procuring envelopes to mail his seed implies that his abrupt departure from the mill indicates sexual disappointment—a possibility sharpened by Old Bach's assistant, a heartless boy ironically named Cupid. The story's crude gynecological imagery also reflects anxieties about female sexuality, even as the tale implies an antipathy toward efforts to control or supplant it. Melville seems cognizant of the reproductive logic undergirding gender and sexual norms, even as his story is unwilling or unable to imagine people living virtuously and happily beyond them. The first half of "The Paradise of Bachelors and the Tartarus of Maids" emphasizes the pleasures of bachelorhood but hints at its degeneracy, while the second half shows that women working outside of home and marriage risk losing their life force. As in other Melville texts, it is hard to disentangle Melville from his narrator, though the seedman's enjoyment of the Paradise of Bachelors and his flight from the Tartarus of Maids can suggest some self-awareness and even self-critique from an author who seldom wrote about women but was attuned to aspects of queerness.

Chapter 7
Pushed and pulled to poetry

Melville was both pushed and pulled toward poetry. Following the disastrous receptions of *Pierre* and *The Confidence-Man*, and despite some limited success with short stories, Melville in the late 1850s moved away from fiction—the genre that had defined his art and career but had become increasingly frustrating for him. Part of the problem had always been genre itself. Beginning with early experimentation and culminating with satire and quarrelsome metacommentary, Melville never comfortably settled into the conventions of nineteenth-century fiction.

He also experienced diminishing returns on multiple fronts. Financially, the earnings from his writings dwindled to the point where he depended on his father-in-law for support. Artistically, he may have exhausted his desire or capacity to innovate fictional forms. Emotionally, he seemed less willing to countenance readers who did not appreciate his originality or iconoclasm, and though he privately and publicly expressed disdain for the book industry, his declining reputation was demoralizing. As the work of writing novels took its toll on his health, family members worried about his sanity and the well-being of Lizzie. In 1857 Melville told a relative that he was giving up writing, and to many it must have seemed so.

Yet Melville's retreat from the public was gradual. In the late 1850s he lectured on travel and Roman statuary, though the charisma that he frequently displayed in social settings did not translate to success on the stage. In 1860 he failed to find a publisher for a book-length manuscript of poems, and in 1866 he published *Battle-Pieces*, a collection of Civil War verse that addressed a national audience on the dominant issues of the day. A decade later, he called his epic poem *Clarel* (1876) "eminently adapted for unpopularity," but he nonetheless released it for public consumption, even if sales, as predicted, were grim. It was not until the privately circulated *John Marr and Other Sailors* (1888) and *Timoleon* (1891) that Melville seems to have finally relinquished his hope of finding a contemporary readership beyond his family and friends.

Indeed, Melville's focus on verse in the late 1850s was not necessarily a renunciation of popularity. Poetry in the nineteenth century was less profitable than fiction, but it was highly respected, widely circulated, and some genres attracted large readerships, particularly pious, sentimental, and patriotic verse that was easily read and recited. Melville did not write such accessible poetry, preferring highbrow themes, layered and ambiguous meanings, learned allusions, rough rhythms, and dense syntax. He also no longer needed income from writing after becoming a US Custom House inspector in 1866, thus freeing him from the pressures of the literary market and allowing him to pursue his dedication to verse.

Always an omnivorous reader, Melville had been a longtime fan of poetry, and he began studying it seriously in the late 1850s. As he reimagined himself as a poet, his book purchases and marginalia show him reading more methodically and registering a range of influences—from classical literature (including verse), to the history of British poetry (especially Spenser and Milton), to nineteenth-century poets (such as Wordsworth, Byron, Tennyson, Robert Browning, Matthew Arnold, and less remembered figures of the time). Melville also sought out aesthetic writings from theorists and practical critics, including commentators on the visual arts (he was especially drawn to painting and sculpture). Melville was not a poetic innovator to the same degree as his contemporaries Walt Whitman and Emily Dickinson, but his verse is distinctive in both content and form. Though he remains best known as an author of fiction, he spent a larger portion of his life writing poetry.

Civil War verse

As suggested by its title, *Battle-Pieces and Aspects of the War* is not a unified book. The collection consists largely of short lyrics and elegies told from manifold perspectives, though it also includes three longer verse narratives and a prose "Supplement" that anticipates the post–Civil War era. Most of the poems are about battles (on land and sea), as well as soldiers (from both the Union and Confederacy), but some are set on the home front, focus on noncombatants, or are abstract to the point of allegory. Much of the collection proceeds chronologically, though it feels less like a history of events and more like an extended reflection in the aftermath of the war. An introductory note states that the "moods" of the book are "variable, and at times widely at variance." Intensely felt but also ambivalent, reverential as well as iconoclastic, fearful and hopeful for the future of America, attentive to both beauty and suffering—*Battle-Pieces* is a richly conflicted book that foregrounds its own uncertainties about the most divisive years in US history.

In some of his fictions, Melville joined other antebellum writers in anticipating nationwide violence over slavery. But no one foresaw the carnage of the Civil War, which lasted four years and included the deaths of over 600,000 soldiers (2 percent of the nation's total population, which would be equivalent to almost seven million casualties today). Generally speaking, the Civil War was not a subject for notable fiction until decades after its end, but it immediately inspired much poetry—not only Whitman's rousing *Drum-Taps* (1865) and Dickinson's oblique verse, but also more popular works by Henry Timrod, Julia Ward Howe, George Henry Boker, and Thomas Buchanan Read. Such verse often presented heroic feats, tragic deaths, and providential designs viewed with moral and political clarity. Part of poetry's cultural work at the time was to mourn the dead and move toward national reconciliation by ascribing order and meaning to the war.

By contrast, *Battle-Pieces* confronts the chaos and potential nihilism of the conflict. Melville makes his loyalties explicit by dedicating the volume to fallen Union soldiers, and some of his poems depict Southern secession and slavery as errors, crimes, and sins. That said, the collection more frequently dwells on the uncertainties of the war. The opening poem, "The Portent," describes the hanging body of John Brown, who was sanctified by abolitionists as a martyr and reviled by his opponents as a terrorist. With its truncated rhythms and slanted rhymes, Melville's terse, unnerving poem presents a "Weird John Brown" whose anguish "none can draw" and whose face, like the future, remains hidden. "Weird" can mean both strange and fateful; as a portent, Brown signals a coming calamity but remains a prophet without a discernible prophecy. The next three poems in *Battle-Pieces*—"Misgivings," "The Conflict of Convictions," and "Apathy and Enthusiasm"—further dramatize contrasting perspectives and turbulent emotions on the eve of the war. Recalling a time before sectional allegiances hardened in the crucible of combat, *Battle-Pieces* begins with a nation unsure of what to think and how to feel.

Such ambivalence continues within and between poems even after violence and loss become realities. Memorializing one of the war's bloodiest battles, "Shiloh" lyrically describes swallows "[s]kimming lightly, wheeling still" over a field of wounded men, "the parched ones stretched in pain." When the poem says of them, "Fame or country least their care: / (What like a bullet can undeceive!)," Melville challenges narratives of patriotic glory while still honoring the sacrifice of soldiers. Similarly, "Malvern Hill" sets the horror of war under the pastoral shade of cypress and elms, while "The College Colonel" contrasts the naivety of a victory parade with the terrible but unnamable truth learned by the disabled protagonist. More hopefully, the "geometric beauty" of warships in "Dupont's Round Fight" reflects an orderly, law-governed universe, but "The Armies of the Wilderness" depicts the confusion of battle and limitations of art: "None can narrate that strife in the pines." The fog of war also pervades "The Scout toward Aldie," a long poem that begins as a romantic adventure but ends with senseless death (and is loosely based on Melville's brief war experience when he accompanied Union cavalry on a scouting mission).

Even poems that offer some closure—some moral insight or emotional poise—leave residues of doubt. "Lee in the Capitol," *Battle-Pieces'* penultimate poem, hints that any definitive summation of the war is willful to the point of delusion. Tracing the surrender of Robert E. Lee and his subsequent testimony before Congress, the poem voices a host of fears: Will white Southerners accept their defeat? Will they exact retribution on recently freed Black Americans? Will their resentment, coupled with Northern punishment, lead to another war? "Lee in the Capitol" answers with seeming optimism but echoes the unnerving language of "The Portent":

> Brave though the Soldier, grave his plea—
> > Catching the light in the future's skies,
> Instinct disowns each darkening prophecy:
> > Faith in America never dies;
> Heaven shall the end ordained fulfill,
> We march with Providence cheery still.

After all of *Battle-Pieces'* misgivings, bloodshed, grief, and failures to predict the future, "cheery" confidence seems utterly inadequate to what has come before.

Battle-Pieces shares the skepticism of Melville's fiction in that the search for meaning is both imperative and impossible, though the "Supplement" to the book represents Melville's most explicit political commentary. He calls slavery a "curse," blames the Civil War on slaveholders, and depicts the Union's victory as just. But he also joins centrist leaders of the time who warned the North not to celebrate too passionately or seek retribution on the South. In a volatile political moment, "Supplement" attempts to strike a careful and perhaps impossible balance: patriotism need not be partisan, religion need not be zealotry, compromise need not abandon moral principles, and conviction need not lead to self-righteousness. Skepticism can risk ethical and political paralysis, but—for better and for worse—it can also justify an anti-dogmatic moderation. "Supplement" ends with the word "Humanity," but unlike the last line of "Bartleby, the Scrivener," there is no hint of irony.

How inclusively *Battle-Pieces* invokes humanity can foreshadow the failures of postbellum America. "Supplement" acknowledges that Black Americans deserve sympathy, but it focuses primarily on the fate of white Southerners, "who stand nearer to us in nature." In "'Formerly a Slave,'" *Battle-Pieces* briefly addresses the future of recently freed African Americans, but it does so by ruminating on the "idealized" portrait of a Black woman, not an actual person. The poem describes the figure as "Sibylline" (mysterious and prophetic), though it concludes—too quickly and conveniently—that the woman is "benign" and brings "cheer." Another poem, "The Swamp Angel," metaphorically presents a more powerful and vengeful Black figure, but *Battle-Pieces* remains primarily interested in white Americans, even as it dwells on struggles shared by a range of people—uncertainty and loss, the inscrutability of Providence, the difficulty of representing traumatic experience, the challenge of reconciling a nation riven by animosities, and the problem of assembling coherent memories from disparate aspects of the war.

People usually prefer unambiguous narratives, and reviews of *Battle-Pieces* on the whole were poor. Politically, some commentators condemned the book as too sympathetic to the South. Poetically, some praised the vigor of Melville's verse but more often found it inharmonious. It is not that Melville had no ear for lyric beauty ("Shiloh" shows as much), and poems such as "The March to the Sea" swing, at least initially, with a robust rhythm. But *Battle-Pieces* generally prefers a rough and unadorned poetic style commensurate with Melville's knotted views of the war. William Dean Howells wrote of the collection, "Mr. Melville's work possesses the negative virtues of originality in such degree that it not only reminds you of no poetry you have read, but of no life you have known." Howells wanted a more familiar, more relatable verse, but as much as Melville hoped for national reconciliation, *Battle-Pieces* failed—or more accurately, refused—to present a unified or unifying vision of the war.

Cross-bearing

Readers relatively new to Melville should not rush to take up *Clarel*, a poem of almost 18,000 lines that took Melville over five years to write and remains his most demanding work. As an epic chiefly concerned with the intellectual and emotional challenges of Christian belief, *Clarel* has been compared to Dante's *Divine Comedy* (1321) and Milton's *Paradise Lost* (1667), though it also dwells on modern issues such as the decline of faith in an age of science and cultural pluralism. *Clarel*'s erudite references, archaic diction, and inverted syntax make it wonderfully strange though also difficult to parse, particularly if the length of the poem tempts readers to hurry through it. With patience and some guidance, *Clarel*'s brilliance and pleasures begin to make themselves known. Readers may appreciate Walter Bezanson's edition of the poem, which includes a chronology, maps, notes, and a helpful index of characters.

Clarel is constituted by 150 cantos divided into four parts, and its plot is simple enough. Clarel, an American theology student, suffers a crisis of faith as he visits Palestine (also called the Holy Land and the Levant), where he falls in love with Ruth, an American-born Jew who has settled in Jerusalem with her converted father, Nathan. After Nathan is killed, Clarel visits the Jordan River, the Dead Sea, Mar Saba monastery, and Bethlehem—a standard itinerary for Western travelers of the time, and one reflecting Melville's 1857 visit to Palestine, which he chronicled in a journal on which *Clarel* draws. On his pilgrimage, Clarel meets a host of diverse characters as his idealized feelings for Ruth override his religious doubts, but he returns to Jerusalem only to find that she has died before he vanishes into obscurity.

The main impetus of *Clarel* is not really about romance so much as finding meaning and succor in a world of waning religious assurance. Melville often viewed religious institutions with suspicion, and his novels increasingly challenge Christian orthodoxies. *Clarel* follows this pattern, though more deeply than any of Melville's books explore faith as a theological, historical, global, and emotional question, while the immense learning and stubborn interrogations of the poem show Melville to be as dedicated a religious thinker as any literary figure of his time. Two months before Melville arrived in Jerusalem, Hawthorne met him in Liverpool and wrote of his wayward friend: "If he were a religious man, he would be one of the most truly religious and reverential."

Much of *Clarel* contains religious discussions among Clarel's fellow tourists and pilgrims. His most consistent companions are Derwent (an Anglican priest with liberal views), Vine (an aesthete who may be based on Hawthorne), and Rolfe (a rover obsessed with religion and lacking settled beliefs). Rolfe may most resemble Melville, but the many dialogues of *Clarel* make it hard to ascribe a stable authorial point of view, especially given the poem's many secondary characters, including Nehemiah (an evangelical

American), Mortmain (an idealistic Swede-turned-misanthrope), Margoth (a Jewish geologist with atheistic tendencies), Ungar (a mixed-race white and Native American Catholic who fought for the Confederacy), and Djalea (the party's Druze guide who carries quiet authority).

No single perspective dominates *Clarel*. No single religion, ethnicity, race, or nation is vested with privileged access to truth. The poem is best versed in Christian traditions and focuses on Western characters, but it has a relatively cosmopolitan outlook that engages various Christian denominations, Judaism, Islam, and (to a lesser degree) Hinduism and Buddhism. *Clarel* reflects stereotypes of the time, such as the fatalistic Muslim, the militant Turk, and the Jewess as an object of attraction. But, as Hilton Obenzinger has argued, Melville rejected the belief of some of his contemporaries that a Judeo-Christian restoration of Palestine would affirm America's providential destiny. On the contrary, as William Potter has emphasized, *Clarel* draws on the emerging field of comparative religion, which tended to view all creeds as legitimate belief systems sharing similar narrative structures and values.

Clarel dramatizes a range of religious comportments, some of which are more compelling than others, but none adequate in and of itself. Younger characters evade theological conundrums by focusing on earthly pleasures. Margoth has no need for the hypothesis of God, though his scientific materialism is narrow. At the other extreme, Nehemiah holds fast to his Bible with visionary certitude, while Mortmain and Ungar stubbornly insist on the irredeemable fallenness of the world. Strong beliefs in *Clarel* tend to look dogmatic in the context of so many faiths and doubts, but even characters more amendable to pluralism are subject to critique. Vine is a thoughtful, ironic observer who remains emotionally distant. Derwent's latitudinarianism is more congenial but also seems superficial. The voluble Rolfe is open-minded and profound, though he may be more interested in discussion than finding a creed by which to live, as if speculation is less a mode of truth-seeking and more a habit or end in itself. As in William Butler Yeats's "The Second Coming" (1920), another poem that measures the decline of faith by looking back twenty centuries to the deserts around Bethlehem, characters in *Clarel* either lack conviction or are too full of passionate intensity.

For his part, the roots of Clarel's struggle with faith are never definitively named, though like many Victorian Protestant intellectuals, his "[e]strangement" is strikingly "modern." One of his problems is that biblical stories cannot be verified or even enlivened two thousand years after their supposed fact. Holy sites in *Clarel* occasionally arouse piety, but often they are dubious or fail to move visitors, especially when presented by overweening guides such as those in the commercialized Bethlehem. There are no T-shirt vendors or people taking selfies, but the birthplace of Jesus feels like a tourist trap. Nature sometimes provides religious inspiration in the mode of Romanticism, but much of *Clarel*'s landscape is too barren and alien for the pilgrims to feel close to the origins of Christianity. Nor does learning bolster faith when *Clarel* mentions David Friedrich Strauss, who in seeking to prove the accuracy of the Bible threatened to replace spiritual wonder with disenchanting historicism and empiricism. In a similar vein, *Clarel* returns periodically to "the wars of Faith and Science," referring to discoveries by Darwin and others, who undermined beliefs in a biblical timeline and benevolent nature designed by God. Perhaps the most enduring obstacle to Clarel's faith remains religious pluralism. With so many earnest people following so many different creeds, how can anyone maintain their conviction?

Yet another problem for Clarel is sexual anxiety, for he seems covertly attracted to Vine and more explicitly worries about his passion for Ruth. On his last night in Mar Saba, he meets a merchant from Lyon who sensually sings about the lilies of the valley. That night, Clarel dreams of standing between the lilies of the merchant and the desert of a celibate monk, until "clasping arms" reminiscent of Ruth save him from either extreme. When he wakes, "[H]e knew organic change, / Or felt, at least that change was working." Ruth, or perhaps human intimacy more generally, comes to figure a synthesis of heaven and earth that gives the formerly passive Clarel new clarity and direction. Though initially troubled by Jerusalem's religious diversity, he ultimately hastens back to the city to find Ruth.

Pluralistic love seems poised to win the day, until Clarel finds Ruth's people burying her. Hours before, he had upbraided himself for leaving Ruth after her father's death, but now his grief turns into rage against the mourning Jews and the world itself:

> And ye—your tribe—'twas *ye* denied
> Me access to this virgin's side
> In bitter trial: take my curse!—
> O blind, blind, barren universe!

Clarel is not a happy book. Each of its four parts ends with a death, and many of the lengthy interactions between characters conclude with differences of perspective and temperament that preclude enduring sympathy. Like so many of Melville's works, the poem tends toward isolation.

And yet *Clarel* has moments of powerful connection—shared grief for Nehemiah's passing in the wilderness, a wine-fueled celebration in Mar Saba, symphonic organ music in Bethlehem, and finally the Via Crucis of Jerusalem. After Clarel's xenophobic resentment spirals into an existential fugue, his crisis unfolds across Holy Week and culminates in a canto titled "Easter" that begins: "But on the third day Christ arose." The implication is that Clarel's faith may undergo its own resurrection, though the poem ends not with his redemption but instead with the crowds on the Via Crucis—the road that Christ walked to his crucifixion, and one marked by the Stations of the Cross. Such coordinates are decidedly Christian, and yet the canto ends with a procession of

"Jews," "monks," "slaves," "Turk soldiers," "Strangers and exiles," an "Edomite," "Moslem dames," "Arab girls," and even the "patient ass" who was part of Clarel's pilgrimage.

Without specifying the complex histories and dynamics between the different communities inhabiting Jerusalem, *Clarel* concludes its pluralistic panorama:

> In varied forms of fate they wend—
> Or man or animal, 'tis one:
> Cross-bearers all, alike they tend
> And follow, slowly follow on.

A figure lagging behind is surely Clarel, but he is still a part of the procession. It is hard to say whether he has found some comfort among the other lives around him, but the passage implies a set of humanistic claims—that our affiliations are not solely based on similar identities, shared beliefs, or romantic love, that the most meaningful pluralism does something more than simply tolerate difference, and that what most powerfully binds all people together are the sufferings borne together and apart.

The "Epilogue" to *Clarel* may or may not extend such sentiments and can stand as something of a litmus test for how one generally responds to Melville in matters of hope and skepticism. The "Epilogue" asserts that "Luther's day" may lengthen to "Darwin's year," but the claims of faith are not foreclosed, for if modern knowledge casts doubt on religion, when "[t]he light is greater, hence the shadow more." Heaven remains a possibility, and though Clarel's heart is "ill-resigned," *Clarel* itself concludes with symbols of redemption—"the crocus budding through the snow," "a swimmer rising from the deep," and (in a poem about the fragility of intimacy) a "burning secret" revealed. Some readers regard *Clarel*'s ending as too facile to be entirely earnest, but those who find themselves moved by the "Epilogue" may sense an elevation of hard-won, never fully achieved belief over irony and iconoclasm. Or we might find ourselves undecided in the end, beginning where Clarel and *Clarel* started—with uncertainty, itself a precondition for faith.

The later verse

Melville's poems that appear after *Clarel* are deep cuts worthy of attention. One way to approach them is to take individual poems as examples of Melville's enduring obsessions—life at sea, aesthetic form, intimacy and isolation, relations between humans and nature, the passing and presence of history. Another way to approach the later poems is to emphasize their arrangements in books that reflect changes across Melville's career—from questing toward nostalgia, from world-making toward observation, from subjectivity toward selflessness, from public toward private orientations, and from works of immense scope and ambition toward short lyrics that find wonder in everyday life. Compared with *Battle-Pieces* and *Clarel*, *John Marr and Other Sailors*, *Timoleon*, and *Weeds and Wildings* are more miscellaneous books, though Melville roughly organizes each around central themes and moods.

John Marr and Other Sailors is a bittersweet collection that begins by memorializing men of the sea, most notably John Marr, an old tar who finds no fellowship in his landlocked life and dwells on his lost shipmates. The adventures, camaraderie, and thumping language of sailors are wistfully rendered in the book, while the loneliness and dangers of sea life are marked less by the dramatic pain of trauma and more by the ache of absence. Poems such as "The Maldive Shark" and "Pebbles" explore human links to a vaguely known natural world. This tracks a resignation of personal identity and even a kind of eschatological return to a more elemental state of being, though for the most part *John Marr and Other Sailors* feels written by an author yearning for the past.

Timoleon is a more intellectual collection that probably includes poems from the manuscript of verse that Melville failed to publish in 1860. Much of the volume draws on Melville's Mediterranean travels in 1856 and 1857, experiences that he discussed in his unsuccessful lecture, "Statues of Rome" (1857). Many nineteenth-century readers were obsessed with Greek and Roman antiquity, and Melville in his fiction often engages the political, philosophical, and artistic legacies of classicism. As Cody Marrs has emphasized, *Timoleon* focuses on objects in which "unlike things must meet and mate." Examples include moss-covered structures, shattered vases covered with spiderwebs, and panoramas that mix land and sea. Melville lauds what one poem calls "The All-in-All," a kind of unity that, like classical architecture, almost seamlessly combines disparate elements. Dedicated to the painter Elihu Vedder, *Timoleon* contains many poems that reflect Melville's immersion in the visual arts and history of aesthetics.

Timoleon also contains poems of longing that are profoundly if ambiguously personal. In what has been read as a coded expression of Melville's feelings for Hawthorne, "After the Pleasure Party" is voiced by a female speaker who appeals to wisdom as a balm for sexual frustration. Similarly, "Monody" mourns a relationship begun in love and ended with estrangement, whether the elegy refers to Hawthorne, Melville's son Malcolm, or some other nexus of regret. Like its titular poem about family conflict and exile, *Timoleon* is held together by a sense of personal and historical loss—of beauties that prove unsustainable, of intimacies unfulfilled, and of feeling out of place and time.

In addition to uncollected poems and prose pieces, Melville left a more or less completed manuscript of verse when he died in 1891. Later titled *Weeds and Wildings Chiefly*, the book is composed mainly of short poems about flora, fauna, and domestic scenes. It also includes a handful of prose introductions such as a tender dedication to Melville's wife and a sketch, "Rip Van Winkle's Lilac," that imagines natural and artistic beauty flourishing in inhospitable conditions. The relative simplicity of many of the poems in *Weeds and Wildings* should not disguise their nuance and range. Melville reflects on aging, death, the tenuousness of beauty, and the challenges of interpretation. He expresses love and sexual desire in his poems about roses and often writes in surprisingly playful and tranquil moods. The final couplet of the last poem, "L'envoi," suggests that restless seeking and marital turmoil can give way to satisfactions undiminished by regret: "Wiser in relish, if sedate / Come gray-beards to their roses late." It is as if Melville finally learned some lessons from his self-destructive, ever-questing characters. *Weeds and Wildings* can also serve as a reminder that even in his grandest works, Melville quietly appreciates moments of intimacy and the intricacies of the natural world.

A ragged conclusion:
Billy Budd

Billy Budd, Sailor is considered Melville's last work, and it plays a definitive role in narratives of his life and career. During his last decades, Melville read widely, collected prints and engravings, and wrote poetry that he published privately. His circle grew smaller as friends and family passed, but he also met and corresponded with old and new acquaintances and seems to have found some domestic happiness. When Melville died from heart disease in 1891, only a few obituaries memorialized him as a long-ago author of maritime fiction. Among the unpublished papers that he left behind was the manuscript of a novella stored in a tin bread box. Melville had written a conclusion (or more accurately, a set of conclusions) to the narrative, though annotations and fragments show that he continued to revise the manuscript up until his death. His wife and subsequent editors have assembled *Billy Budd* into a work that stands as Melville's final achievement—one that looks back on the body of his writings and points forward toward his ultimate fame.

In and of itself, *Billy Budd* is a story of moral ambiguity and interpretive possibilities. In the aftermath of the French Revolution, during a time of conflict between Britain and France, the handsome, innocent, beloved Billy Budd is taken from his merchant ship, *The Rights-of-Man*, and forced to serve on the British warship *Bellipotent* (a legal practice known as impressment). For reasons that remain mysterious, the *Bellipotent*'s master-at-arms Claggart falsely accuses Billy of plotting a mutiny, and when Captain Vere summons both men before him, Billy's stutter precludes him from defending himself. Instead, he impulsively punches Claggart, unintentionally killing him and instigating a trial in which Vere, despite believing in Billy's innocence, leads a tribunal that condemns him to death. Billy and Vere then share an unnarrated meeting that ends in some kind of mutual sympathy, and just before his strangely beautiful hanging, Billy's last words are "God bless Captain Vere!" Soon after, Vere dies from battle wounds murmuring Billy's name.

As a text that revisits many of Melville's major themes, *Billy Budd* can serve as a summation of his work. Like *Typee*, *Omoo*, and *Mardi*, the novella stages an encounter between unspoiled innocence and the ineluctable forces of Western civilization. Billy is called a "superior *savage*" and compared to a "Tahitian" before he is doomed by the conniving Claggart and rule-driven rationalist Vere. As in Melville's Pacific Island novels, natural goodness does not survive the corruptions of modernity, even if Vere—more explicitly than Melville's early narrators—agonizes over his role in the ending of innocence.

Billy Budd resembles *Redburn* and *White-Jacket* when it dwells on the inequalities of shipboard life and social injustice more generally. The novella resonates with specific political contexts—the *Nore* and *Spithead* mutinies of 1797 (both mentioned in the text), the 1842 hanging of mutineers on the USS *Somers* (where one of Melville's cousins served as an officer), the Haymarket Affair of 1886 (in which anarchists and labor activists were hung after an unfair trial), and the suppression of speech in the Reconstruction era (most gruesomely figured by lynching). Like "Benito Cereno," *Billy Budd* is set at the end of the eighteenth century, but in drawing on historical and contemporary injustices, it questions the theoretical legitimacy of authority.

Many readers take seriously Vere's ethical dilemma: execute an innocent man who violated the letter of the law, or exonerate him (or defer judgment) and risk mutiny in a time of war. Vere prioritizes duty and practical consequences over his conscience and convictions, a choice that readers might decry while still taking Vere to act in good faith. Vere may even suffer as much as the fatally flawed hero he condemns, making *Billy Budd* a richly tragic story comparable to Sophocles's *Antigone* and a fit subject for the Benjamin Britten's operatic adaption with a libretto by E. M. Forster. By focusing on the suffering shared by leaders and subordinates alike, *Billy Budd* presents Melville's most sympathetic portrait of a captain and is for many a deeply humanistic narrative in which the rebellious Melville makes peace with the powers that be.

Yet some readers discern an ironic critique in which Vere and a narrator who does not speak for Melville try and fail to justify the actions of the captain. In this account, Melville prefers Thomas Paine's *Rights of Man* (1791) to the more conservative political theories of Thomas Hobbes and Edmund Burke. Vere only appears to be righteously guided by duty, logic, and law, for Billy's trial is overdetermined from the start, thus exposing the self-vindicating ideology of a system all too ready to sacrifice human rights in the interests of war and control. Like *Redburn* and *White-Jacket*—as well as "Bartleby, the Scrivener" and "The Encantadas"—*Billy Budd* simultaneously dramatizes abuses of power, the claims of political order, and the tragic imperatives of moral action under conditions of uncertainty.

In doing so, the novella follows many Melville texts by tracing its sociopolitical concerns to philosophical and theological conundrums. Like *Moby-Dick* and *Pierre*, the novella asks us to ask: Is the world governed by natural laws, universal principles, and providential designs? If so, how might such truths be known? And if they prove beyond our knowledge or do not exist at all, how can social structures, moral systems, and rational arguments justify themselves? After witnessing Billy kill Claggart, Vere faces the gap between heavenly and human law. "Struck dead by an angel of God!" he marvels, "Yet the angel must hang!" As scholars of literature and law have shown, the dilemma of deciding Billy's fate involves Vere's application of martial law and his handling of the trial proceedings. *Billy Budd* also depicts the struggles faced by judges when positive law dictates unjust outcomes, a problem that Melville's father-in-law experienced when he enforced the Fugitive Slave Law.

For readers focused more on moral than juridical approaches, judgment in *Billy Budd* inevitably depends on the motives and natures of Claggart, Budd, and Vere. Yet as Susan Mizruchi and Sharon Cameron have emphasized, the main characters of *Billy Budd* lack transparency and consistency. Billy's innocence and lack of self-reflection allow for only a superficial understanding of his nature, and his striking of Claggart without seeming intention raises the question of free will and whether Billy, whom Vere calls a "Fated boy," should be held responsible for his actions. For his part, Claggart's animus toward Billy may be driven by frustrated homosexual desire, an argument made by Eve Kosofsky Sedgwick. But it can also be attributed to metaphysical explanations such as "[n]atural depravity" and "the mystery of iniquity," or physiological causes that the novella calls "something defective or abnormal in the constitution and blood." We have more access to Vere's interiority, but he remains a rationalist swayed by emotion and a rule follower who breaks military protocols. As in *The Confidence-Man*, Melville refuses to create the kind of consistent, clearly motivated characters typically expected from fiction. Indeed, *Billy Budd*'s metacritical asides about its "matter of writing" sound like those of *The Confidence-Man* in that Melville frustrates desires for "realism" as it was understood by readers of the time.

While *Billy Budd* recalls the social, philosophical, and aesthetic iconoclasm of Melville's previous fictions, it can also evoke aspects of his poetry—*Battle-Pieces*' skeptical yet redemptive depictions of sacrifice in war (including the hanging of John Brown), *Clarel*'s wrestling with theological paradoxes involving free will and theodicy, and the self-conscious nostalgia of *John Marr and Other Sailors* (a collection that at one point included "Billy in the Darbies," the ballad that ends *Billy Budd*). One pleasure of immersing oneself in Melville's writings is recognizing continuities across his work, and *Billy Budd* can provide a basis for a relatively comprehensive account of Melville's art.

Yet what most powerfully positions the novella as a retrospective on Melville's career is its return to the genre that made him famous and continues to define his reputation today. Forty years after *Moby-Dick* ended Melville's run of sea novels, *Billy Budd* shows the enduring pull of maritime life on his imagination, even if Melville acknowledges in the novella that some of his interests have "fallen out of date." The return to origins at the end of life is a trope that Melville leverages in *Israel Potter*. That the manuscript of *Billy Budd* was unpublished at Melville's death reinforces a related narrative of his life—the story of a once-popular genius misunderstood by readers, persecuted by reviewers, battered by an inhospitable book market, and relegated to obscurity before unexpected and belated fame.

To reclaim *Billy Budd* as a deathbed masterpiece is to enjoy both the gravitas of tragedy and the pleasures of redemption. Melville's mature writing gives little reason for optimism, but as bleak as his vision can be, figures like Redburn, White-Jacket, Ishmael, and Clarel offer tenuous hope through survival and perseverance. Just as *Billy Budd* found its way from bread box to canon, so too did the nearly forgotten Melville rise, as if Billy's Christ-like death prefigures the arc of Melville's posthumous reputation: "[He] ascended; and, ascending, took the full rose of the dawn." Pockets of dedicated readers in Britain and America began rediscovering Melville's work around the time of his death. In the 1920s the "Melville Revival" among scholars laid the foundations for the canonization of his writings, which was fully established by the

1950s and, unlike other major figures of nineteenth-century American literature, has not declined to this day. The story of Herman Melville's redemption is satisfying and not untrue, but as he writes near the end of *Billy Budd*, "Truth uncompromisingly told will always have its ragged edges."

True to form, *Billy Budd* has multiple endings, each of which can serve as a kind of conclusion to a very short introduction to Melville. Billy's death is so lyrically described and his relationship with Vere so apparently sympathetic that it is tempting to read in Melville's last work a setting aside of iconoclastic rage at an inexplicably unjust world and to find instead a movement toward acceptance based on shared suffering and compassion. Vere the disciplinarian and Billy the orphan are likened to father and son. Perhaps Melville, who seldom writes about fathers except as absent figures, finally imagines in *Billy Budd* some succor for his painful past.

Yet *Billy Budd* does not end with reconciliation and the relationship between Billy and Vere. When the ship's purser and surgeon wonder why Billy's body did not spasm during his hanging, their narrow materiality disallows anything that smacks of "the imaginative and metaphysical." Here Melville renews hostilities with a scientific, capitalistic age that marginalized his artistic and intellectual commitments. In this reading, the iconoclast remains unmollified. Nor does Billy's death reconcile Melville to the *Bellipotent*'s authoritarian system, for Vere and his officers must use "[t]rue martial discipline" to suppress the mutinous mood of the crew in the aftermath of Billy's execution.

For all the Christ-like imagery and symbolic order of its climax, *Billy Budd* does not conclude with peace or acceptance as the multiple meanings of Billy's death continue to proliferate. Vere's last words—"Billy Budd, Billy Budd"—can suggest enduring love and consecration but, like the conclusion to "Bartleby, the Scrivener," also hypocrisy and guilt. The naval newspaper that misrepresents Billy's actions and makes a victim of Claggart extends Melville's critique of social control and suggests that he continued to resent the print industry even after he left professional writing behind. More truthful, but also not beyond skepticism, are the sympathetic stories about Billy's death that circulate among seaman by ballad and yarn. For an author who had his most formative experiences as a sailor and returned to

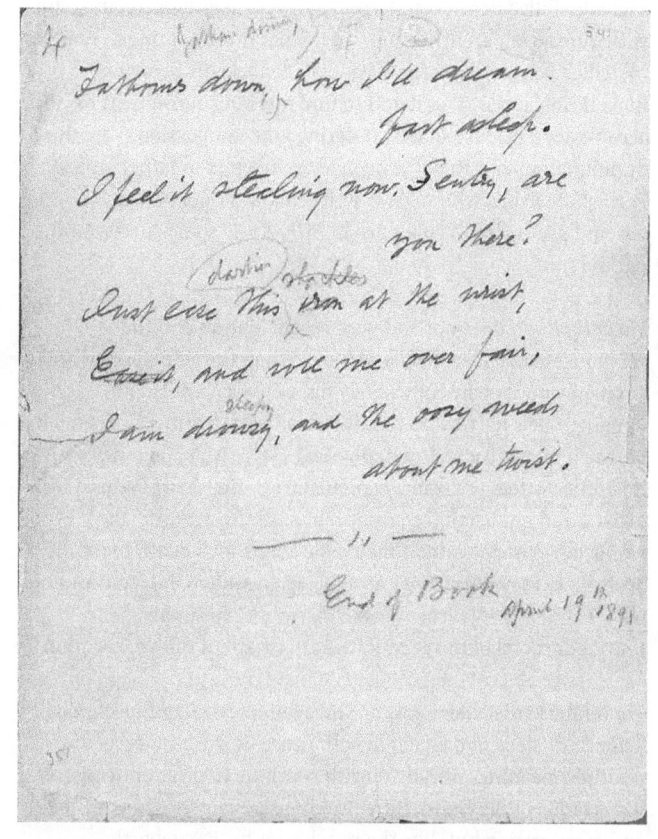

10. The final manuscript page of *Billy Budd*, found in a bread box at Melville's death in 1891.

memories of the sea at the end of his life, it is fitting that Melville concludes his last work with the sailors' song "Billy in the Darbies"—that among its many conclusions, *Billy Budd* gives sailors the last word.

Except that *Billy Budd* has no definitive ending, insofar as Melville never finished revising the manuscript. We do not know precisely when he began *Billy Budd* or when he had largely completed it, but Harrison Hayford and Merton M. Sealts Jr. wonder whether his revisions were a kind of "puttering." Perhaps Melville's inability or unwillingness to complete *Billy Budd* points to his failing powers. Perhaps the novella is not a fitting summation of his work, as if any single text might encompass the immensity of his achievements. Yet Melville's continuing to work on *Billy Budd* may be an apt enough ending, suggesting—despite the disappointments of his career and the imminence of his death—the endurance and even hope of an author who saw the ragged edges of truth and would not write the final word.

References

Chapter 1: A brief biography

Sophia Hawthorne quoted in Raymond M. Weaver, *Herman Melville, Mariner and Mystic* (New York: George H. Doran, 1921), 24.

Andrew Delbanco, *Melville: His World and Work* (New York: Vintage Books, 2006), xxii.

Alexis de Tocqueville, *Democracy in America; and Two Essays on America*, trans. Gerald E. Bevan (1840; New York: Penguin Books, 2003), 64.

Karl Marx and Frederick Engels, *The Communist Manifesto: A Modern Edition* (New York: Verso, 1998), 38.

Hershel Parker, *Herman Melville: A Biography*, vol. 1, *1819–1851* (Baltimore: Johns Hopkins University Press, 2005), 530.

Elizabeth Renker, "Herman Melville, Wife Beating, and the Written Page," *American Literature* 66, no. 1 (March 1994), 123–50.

Nathaniel Hawthorne, *The English Notebooks*, ed. Randall Stewart (New York: Modern Language Association of America, 1941), 432.

Raymond M. Weaver, *Herman Melville, Mariner and Mystic* (New York: George H. Doran, 1921), 349.

William Dean Howells quoted in Edith Wharton, *A Backwards Glance* (New York: Scribner's, 1933), 147.

Chapter 2: Truth, sex, and empire: The Pacific Island novels

Walt Whitman, "Literary News, Notices, Etc.," *Brooklyn Daily Eagle*, April 15, 1846, 2.

John Bryant, *The Fluid Text: A Theory of Revision and Editing for Book and Screen* (Ann Arbor: University of Michigan Press, 2002).

Geoffrey Sanborn, *The Sign of the Cannibal: Melville and the Making of a Postcolonial Reader* (Durham, NC: Duke University Press, 1998).

H. C., "Notices of New Publications," *New York Evangelist*, April 9, 1846, 60.

"Typee: The Traducers of Missions," *Christian Parlor Magazine*, July 1846, 74.

Samuel Otter, *Melville's Anatomies* (Berkeley: University of California Press, 1999).

D. H. Lawrence, *Studies in Classic American Literature*, ed. Ezra Greenspan, Lindeth Vasey, and John Worthen (1923; Cambridge: Cambridge University Press, 2003), 122.

Chapter 3: A moving world: *Redburn* and *White-Jacket*

Herman Melville, *Journals*, ed. Harrison Hayford (Evanston and Chicago: Northwestern University Press and the Newberry Library, 1989), 13.

William H. Gilman, *Melville's Early Life and "Redburn"* (New York: New York University Press, 1951).

Georg Lukács, *The Theory of the Novel: A Historico-Philosophical Essay on the Forms of Great Epic Literature*, trans. Anna Bostock (1920; Cambridge: MIT Press, 1971), 41.

Michael Rogin, *Subversive Genealogy: The Politics and Art of Herman Melville* (Berkeley: University of California Press, 1985).

C. L. R. James, *Mariners, Renegades, and Castaways: The Story of Herman Melville and the World We Live In* (1953; Hanover, NH: Dartmouth College and the University Press of New England, 2001), 4.

Robert S. Levine, "What Is the White American? Race, Emigration, and Nation in Melville's *Redburn*," *J19* 8, no. 1 (Spring 2020), 97–122.

Ralph Ellison, "Twentieth-Century Fiction and the Black Mask of Humanity" (1953), in *Shadow and Act* (New York: Vintage, 1964), 40–41.

Jennifer Greiman, *Melville's Democracy: Radical Figuration and Political Form* (Stanford, CA: Stanford University Press, 2023).

Larry J. Reynolds, "Antidemocratic Emphasis in *White-Jacket*," *American Literature* 48, no. 1 (March 1976), 13–28.

Chapter 4: Four reasons for going to sea in *Moby-Dick*

Henry James, "Preface to *The Tragic Muse* (1890)," in *The Portable Henry James*, ed. John Auchard (New York: Penguin Books, 2004), 477.

Lawrence Buell, *The Dream of the Great American Novel* (Cambridge, MA: Harvard University Press, 2014), 64.

Genesis 16:12 (King James Version of Bible).

The Collected Letters of C. S. Lewis, vol. 3, *Narnia, Cambridge, and Joy, 1950–1963*, ed. Walter Hooper (New York: HarperCollins, 2007), 1169.

C. L. R. James, *Mariners, Renegades, and Castaways: The Story of Herman Melville and the World We Live In* (1953; Hanover, NH: Dartmouth College and the University Press of New England, 2001).

Max Weber, "The Sociology of Charismatic Authority," in *From Max Weber: Essays in Sociology*, ed. and trans. Hans Gerth and C. Wright Mills (New York: Oxford University Press, 1946), 245–52.

F. O. Matthiessen, *American Renaissance: Art and Expression in the Age of Emerson and Whitman* (New York: Oxford University Press, 1941), ix.

Donald Pease, "*Moby-Dick* and the Cold War," in *The American Renaissance Reconsidered*, ed. Walter Benn Michaels and Donald Pease (Baltimore: Johns Hopkins University Press, 1985), 113–55.

Wai-chee Dimock, *Empire for Liberty: Melville and the Poetics of Individualism* (Princeton, NJ: Princeton University Press, 1989).

Jennifer L. Fleissner, *Maladies of the Will: The American Novel and the Modernity Problem* (Chicago: University of Chicago Press, 2022).

Melville and Milton: An Edition and Analysis of Melville's Annotations on Milton, ed. Robin Grey (Pittsburgh: Duquesne University Press, 2004), 51.

Keats to George and Tom Keats, December [21 and 27?] 1817, *Selected Letters*, ed. Robert Gittings (Oxford: Oxford University Press, 2002), 41.

Michael Colacurcio, "'Excessive and Organic Ill': Melville, Evil, and the Question of Politics," *Religion and Literature* 34, no. 3 (Autumn 2002), 1–26.

Newton Arvin, *Herman Melville* (New York: Sloane, 1950), 192.

Chapter 5: Antagonisms: *Pierre, Israel Potter,* and *The Confidence-Man*

"Notices of New Works," *The Albion*, August 21, 1852, 405.

New York Day Book, September 7, 1852.

Nathaniel Hawthorne, *Selected Letters of Nathaniel Hawthorne*, ed. Joel Myerson (Columbus: Ohio State University Press, 2002), xiv.

Nancy Fredericks, "Melville and the Woman's Story," *Studies in American Fiction* 19, no. 1 (Spring 1991), 42.

Branka Arsić, *Passive Constitutions, or 7½ Times Bartleby* (Stanford, CA: Stanford University Press, 2007), 7.

Frederick Douglass, "What to the Slave Is the Fourth of July?" (1852), in *The Portable Frederick Douglass*, ed. John Stauffer and Henry Louis Gates Jr. (New York: Penguin Books, 2016), 202.

Rodrigo Lazo, "Israel Potter Deported," *Leviathan* 22, no. 1 (March 2020), 146–65.

Nina Baym, "Melville's Quarrel with Fiction," *PMLA* 94, no. 5 (October 1979), 909–23.

Samuel Taylor Coleridge, *Biographia Literaria* (1817; Boston: Crocker and Brewster, 1834), 174.

Ralph Waldo Emerson, "Self-Reliance" (1841), in *Essays and Lectures* (New York: Library of America, 1983), 265.

Leslie Marmon Silko, "Indian Hater, Indian Fighter, Indian Killer: Melville's Indictment of the 'New Nation' and the 'New World,'" *Leviathan* 14, no. 1 (March 2012), 94–99.

William James, "The Will to Believe" (1896), in *Writings, 1878–1899* (New York: Library of America, 1992), 469.

Chapter 6: Melville's magazine fiction

Dan E. McCall, *The Silence of Bartleby* (Ithaca, NY: Cornell University Press, 1989).

James Baldwin, *The Fire Next Time* (New York: Dell, 1962), 16.

Eric Sundquist, *To Wake the Nations: Race in the Making of American Literature* (Cambridge, MA: Belknap Press, 1998).

Gayatri Chakravorty Spivak, "Can the Subaltern Speak?" in *Marxism and the Interpretation of Culture*, ed. Cary Nelson and Lawrence Grossberg (Champaign: University of Illinois Press, 1988), 271–313.

Sterling Stuckey, *African Culture and Melville's Art: The Creative Process in "Benito Cereno" and "Moby-Dick"* (New York: Oxford University Press, 2008).

Michael Jonik, *Herman Melville and the Politics of the Inhuman* (Cambridge: Cambridge University Press, 2018).

Christopher Freeburg, *Melville and the Idea of Blackness: Race and Imperialism in Nineteenth-Century America* (Cambridge: Cambridge University Press, 2012).

Chapter 7: Pushed and pulled to poetry

William Dean Howells, "Reviews and Literary Notices," *Atlantic Monthly*, February 1867, 252.

Nathaniel Hawthorne, *The English Notebooks*, ed. Randall Stewart (New York: Modern Language Association of America, 1941), 432.

Hilton Obenzinger, *American Palestine: Melville, Twain, and the Holy Land Mania* (Princeton, NJ: Princeton University Press, 1999).

William Potter, *Melville's "Clarel" and the Intersympathy of Creeds* (Kent, OH: Kent State University Press, 2004).

Cody Marrs, *Melville, Beauty, and American Literary Studies: An Aesthetics in All Things* (Oxford: Oxford University Press, 2023).

A ragged conclusion: *Billy Budd*

Susan Mizruchi, "Cataloging the Creatures of the Deep: 'Billy Budd, Sailor' and the Rise of Sociology," *boundary 2* 17, no. 1 (Spring 1990), 272–304.

Sharon Cameron, *Impersonality: Seven Essays* (Oxford: Oxford University Press, 2007).

Eve Kosofsky Sedgwick, *Epistemology of the Closet* (Berkeley: University of California Press, 1990).

Harrison Hayford and Merton M. Sealts Jr., "Editors' Introduction," in *Billy Budd, Sailor (An Inside Narrative)*, ed. Hayford and Sealts (Chicago: University of Chicago Press, 1962), 34.

Further reading

Melville's writings are widely available, sometimes in low-quality print and digital versions that draw on flawed source texts. The writings of Melville listed at the beginning of this book represent just some of the responsible reading editions available. For scholarly editions, see *The Writings of Herman Melville* published by Northwestern University Press and the Newberry Library. Melville has been studied seriously for over a century, and this book has relied on generations of scholars, only a fraction of whom can be cited. The works listed below include only books focused on Melville and emphasize recent criticism while also including exemplary works from the history of Melville scholarship. For the closest thing to comprehensive bibliographic information, see the Modern Language Association International Bibliography.

Biographies

Arvin, Newton. *Herman Melville*. New York: Sloane, 1950.
Delbanco, Andrew. *Melville: His World and Work*. New York: Vintage Books, 2006.
Leyda, Jay. *The Melville Log: A Documentary Life of Herman Melville, 1819–1891*. 2 vols. Reprint with Supplement. New York: Gordian Press, 1969.
Parker, Hershel. *Herman Melville: A Biography*. 2 vols. Baltimore: Johns Hopkins University Press, 2005.

Critical books

Arsić, Branka. *Passive Constitutions, or 7½ Times Bartleby*. Stanford, CA: Stanford University Press, 2007.

Berthoff, Warner. *The Example of Melville*. Princeton, NJ: Princeton University Press, 1962.

Dimock, Wai-chee. *Empire for Liberty: Melville and the Poetics of Individualism*. Princeton, NJ: Princeton University Press, 1989.

Freeburg, Christopher. *Melville and the Idea of Blackness: Race and Imperialism in Nineteenth-Century America*. Cambridge: Cambridge University Press, 2012.

Greiman, Jennifer. *Melville's Democracy: Radical Figuration and Political Form*. Stanford, CA: Stanford University Press, 2023.

James, C. L. R. *Mariners, Renegades, and Castaways: The Story of Herman Melville and the World We Live In*. 1953; Hanover, NH: Dartmouth College and the University Press of New England, 2001.

Martin, Robert K. *Hero, Captain, and Stranger: Male Friendship, Social Critique, and Literary Form in the Sea Novels of Herman Melville*. Chapel Hill: University of North Carolina Press, 1986.

Milder, Robert. *Exiled Royalties: Melville and the Life We Imagine*. Oxford: Oxford University Press, 2006.

Otter, Samuel. *Melville's Anatomies*. Berkeley: University of California Press, 1999.

Rogin, Michael. *Subversive Genealogy: The Politics and Art of Herman Melville*. Berkeley: University of California Press, 1985.

Sanborn, Geoffrey. *The Sign of the Cannibal: Melville and the Making of a Postcolonial Reader*. Durham, NC: Duke University Press, 1998.

Stuckey, Sterling. *African Culture and Melville's Art: The Creative Process in "Benito Cereno" and "Moby-Dick."* New York: Oxford University Press, 2008.

Recent critical essay collections

These books include the work of many of today's most important scholars working in Melville studies.

Arsić, Branka, and K. L. Evans, eds. *Melville's Philosophies*. London: Bloomsbury, 2017.

Kelley, Wyn, and Christopher Ohge, eds. *A New Companion to Herman Melville*. 2nd ed. London: Wiley-Blackwell, 2022.

Levine, Robert S., ed. *The New Cambridge Companion to Herman Melville*. 2nd rev. ed. Cambridge: Cambridge University Press, 2013.

Marrs, Cody, ed. *The New Melville Studies*. Cambridge: Cambridge University Press, 2019.

Other resources

Bercaw, Mary K. *Melville's Sources*. Evanston, IL: Northwestern University Press, 1987.

Higgins, Brian, and Hershel Parker. *Herman Melville: The Contemporary Reviews*. Cambridge: Cambridge University Press, 1995.

Sealts, Merton M. Jr. *Melville's Reading*. Rev. ed. Columbia: University of South Carolina Press, 1988.

Journal and online resources

Leviathan: A Journal of Melville Studies. Johns Hopkins University Press.

Melville's Electronic Library: A Critical Archive. https://melville.electroniclibrary.org/.

Melville's Marginalia Online. https://melvillesmarginalia.org/.

Index

For the benefit of digital users, indexed terms that span two pages (e.g., 52–53) may, on occasion, appear on only one of those pages.

A

Adams, John 73
Agamben, Giorgio 83
Albany, New York 4–5
Allen, Ethan 65
An Account of the Arctic Regions (Scoresby) 51
Anderson, Laurie 44
animal magnetism 75–6
anthropocentrism 54–5
Antigone (Sophocles) 112
Arnold, Matthew 96–7
Arsić, Branka 71
Arvin, Newton 63–4
Astor, John Jacob 80–1
authoritarianism 50–2
autobiographical fiction 31, 71, 81

B

Baldwin, James 84–6
Bancroft, George 72
Barnum, P. T. 75–6
"Bartleby, The Scrivener" (1853) 79–83
Battle-Pieces (1866) 14–15, 97–101, 107, 113–14
Baym, Nina 74
Beale, Thomas 50
"Benito Cereno" (1855) 79–80, 83–7, 111
Berkshires, Massachusetts 10–12
Bible 10, 46–9, 52–3, 78, 88, 103–4
Bildungsroman 30–3, 36–8, 41–3, 74
Billy Budd (1924) 14–15, 110–17
Boker, George Henry 97–8
Boston, Massachusetts 4, 8
Boston Tea Party 4
Bradstreet, Anne 93
Britten, Benjamin 112
Brontë, Charlotte 31–2
Brown, John 98
Browne, Thomas 10
Browning, Robert 96–7
Buell, Lawrence 45–6
Burke, Edmund 40–1, 112
Byron, George Gordon (Lord) 61–2, 67, 96–7

C

Cameron, Sharon 113
cannibalism 8, 20, 25–6
Cape Horn 8
capitalism 5, 12–13, 23–4, 32–8,
    49–50, 75–6, 80–2, 91–3
Chartist movement 33–4
Chase, Jack 40–1
chattel slavery 25, 28–9, 33–5, 39,
    52–3, 83–7, 97–100
Chavez, Cesar 81
Child, Maria Lydia 72
Christianity
    Billy Budd 114–17
    Clarel 101–7
    Pierre 67–8
    Pacific Island missions 8–9,
        23–4
    Providence and *Moby-Dick*
        60–3
    Readership 8–9, 21, 67–8
"Civil Disobedience" (Thoreau)
    40, 81
Civil War (US) 14–15, 56, 95–101
Clarel (1876) 14–15, 95–6, 101–7
Coetzee, J. M. 44
Colacurcio, Michael 63
Coleridge, Samuel Taylor 58, 74
Columbus, Christopher 85–6
The Communist Manifesto
    (Marx and Engels) 34
Compromise of 1850 52
    see also Fugitive Slave Law
The Confidence-Man (1857), 12–13,
    65, 74–8
Conrad, Joseph 25–6
Cook, James 20
Cooper, James Fenimore 17, 72
Cooper, William 72
The Course of Empire (Cole) 91
The Crater (Cooper) 17
cultural pluralism 26–7, 52–4,
    62–3, 101–7

D

Darwin, Charles 88–9, 106–7
David Copperfield (Dickens) 31–2
Davis, Rebecca Harding 80–1
Delbanco, Andrew 1–4
Deleuze, Gilles 83
democracy 4, 38–41, 50–2, 73
Derrida, Jacques 83
Descartes, Rene 58, 61, 76
Dickens, Charles 9, 31–2, 80–1, 92
Dickinson, Emily 47, 96–8
Dimock, Wai-Chee 53–4
diptychs 91–2
Disraeli, Benjamin 34
domestic fiction 69–70
doppelganger 32–3
Douglass, Frederick 47, 52, 72,
Drum-Taps (Whitman) 97–8

E

Ellison, Ralph 40
Emerson, Ralph Waldo 47, 76–8
empire and imperialism 12–13,
    23–9, 33, 53–6, 89
"The Encantadas" (1854) 79–80,
    87–91
Engels, Friedrich 34
Essex sinking 45

F

family life of Melville 4–7, 10–12,
    14, 30, 67–8, 95–6, 110
Faulkner, William 44
Fern, Fanny 9
Forster, E. M. 112
Foster, George 34
Fourierism 75–6
Fugitive Slave Law 52, 112–13
Fleissner, Jennifer 55–6
Franklin, Bejamin 72
Fredricks, Nancy 71

Freeburg, Cristopher 89
free will 52–3, 61–2, 79–80, 82–3
Frankenstein (Mary Shelley) 61–2
Freud, Anna 18–19
Freud, Sigmund 18–19, 46–7, 68
Fuller, Margaret 9, 34

G

Galapagos Islands 87–8
Gansevoort, Maria (mother) 4–5
Gansevoort, Peter (maternal grandfather) 4
Gaskell, Elizabeth 34, 80–1
Gilman, William 31
Goethe, Johan Wolfgang von 47, 61–2, 67
Greiman, Jennifer 41
Gulliver's Travels (Swift) 28–9

H

Harper and Brothers Publishing 8–9
Harper's Monthly 79
Hawthorne, Nathaniel
  letter to 10–12, 63, 76
  literary market 69
  Liverpool meeting 14, 102
  relationship with 10–12, 45–6, 102–3, 108
Hawthorne, Sophia 1
Hayford, Harrison 117
Haymarket Affair 111
Heart of Darkness (Conrad) 25–6
Hobbes, Thomas 112
homosexuality 22, 48, 56, 67, 91–2, 113
Honolulu, Hawaii 24
Howe, Julia Ward 97–8
Howells, William Dean 15, 101
Hume, David 57–8, 76
"Hungry Forties" 33–4

I

individualism 31–2, 39, 47, 53–6, 78
Industrial Revolution 7, 33–4, 80–1, 93–4
International copyright law 9
Irving, Washington 92
Israel Potter (1855), 12–13, 65, 72–4, 114

J

Jackson, Andrew 5–6, 36, 50–2
James C. L. R. 37, 49–50
James, Henry 45–6
James, William 78
Jane Eyre (Charlotte Brontë) 31–2
Jefferson, Thomas 73
John Marr and Other Sailors (1888) 95–6, 107
Jones, John Paul 72
Jonik, Michael 88–9

K

Kanagawa Treaty 53–4
Kant, Immanuel 58
Keats, John 62
King, Martin Luther, Jr. 81
Know-Nothing Party 37
Kupe, Te Pēhi 53

L

Laertius, Diogenese 76
Lamarck, Jean Baptiste 88
The Last Man (Mary Shelley) 91
Lawrence, D. H. 29
Lazarus, Emma 37
Lazo, Rodrigo 73
Lee, Robert E. 99
Levine, Robert S. 37
Lewis, C. S. 47

Lippard, George 34
Liverpool, England 7, 14, 31–6, 102
Locke, John 57–8
London Labour and the London Poor (Mayhew) 34
loneliness 46–9, 63–4, 78, 82–3, 105, 107
Lowell Mill 93–4
Lukács, Georg 32–3
Luther, Martin 106–7
Lyell, Charles 88

M

Malthus, Thomas 92
Mardi (1849) 9–10, 16, 27–30, 111
Mariners, Renegades, and Castaways (C. L. R. James) 37
Marquesas Islands 8–9, 18, 25
Marryat, Frederick 17–18
Marx, Karl 5, 34, 36–8, 80–1
Mary Barton (Gaskell) 34
Masterman Ready (Marryat) 17
Matthiessen, F. O. 50–2
Mayhew, Henry 34
McCall, Dan 83
Meditations on First Philosophy (Descartes) 76
Melvill, Allan (father) 4–6, 10–12, 71, 115
Melvill, Thomas (paternal grandfather) 4
Melville, Eleanor (granddaughter) 57
Melville, Elizabeth (daughter) 10
Melville, Elizabeth Shaw (wife) 10, 14, 95, 108–9
Melville, Frances (son) 10
Melville, Gansevoort (brother), 5–6, 8–10
Melville, Herman
  canonization 15–16, 50–2, 56, 114–15
  early employment 5–7
  family life 10–12, 14
  family lineage 4
  maritime career 7–8, 31
  mental health 14, 65–6, 95
  literary style 10, 17–18, 28, 45–6, 48–9, 65–6, 69–72, 79–80, 101
  photograph by Rodney Dewey 2
  portrait by Joseph Eaton 3
  struggles with publishing industry 8–15, 17–20, 68–9, 79, 81, 93, 95, 115–17
  U.S. Customs Office 14
Melville, Malcolm (son) 10, 14
Melville, Stanwix (son) 10, 14
Mexican-American War 28–9, 81
Milton, John 10, 61–2, 96–7, 101
mimesis 77
Mitchell, Donald Grant 92
Mizruchi, Susan 113
Moby-Dick (1851), 10–13, 15–16, 44–65, 74, 76, 88–9, 94, 112–13
Mocha-Dick 45
Montaigne, Michel de 76
Morrison, Toni 44
Murray, John 8–9
mutiny 8, 40, 49–50, 110–12

N

Narrative of Arthur Gordon Pym (Poe) 17
The Natural History of the Sperm Whale (Beale) 50
New Bedford, Massachusetts 8, 52
New York City, New York 4, 7, 9–10, 32–4
Nuku Hiva, Marquesas Islands 27

O

Obenzinger, Hilton 103
Omoo (1847) 9–10, 16, 27–30, 111
On the Origin of Species (Darwin) 88
Orientalism 53–4
O'Sullivan, John 23–4

Otter, Samuel 25-6
"Ozymandias" (Percy Bysshe Shelley) 91

P

Paine, Thomas 112
Panic of 1837 5-6, 33-4, 75-6
"The Paradise of Bachelors and the Tartarus of Maids" (1850) 79-80, 91-4
Parker, Hershel 8-9
Pease, Donald 50-2
Pequod Nation 54
Phillips, Katherine 93
phrenology 75-6
The Piazza Tales (1856) 79
Pickwick Papers (Dickens) 92
Pierre (1852) 12-13, 23, 65-71, 73-4, 76, 79, 94-5, 112-13
Plato 58-9, 76
Poe, Edgar Allan 9, 17, 45-6
Pollock, Jackson 44
Potter, William 103
Putnam's Monthly 79

Q

Queen Pomaree (Pōmare IV) 28

R

Ranciére, Jacques 83
Read, Thomas Buchanan 97-8
Redburn (1849) 7, 9-10, 30-9, 42-5, 49, 74, 111-12, 114-15
reform novels 30, 39-40
Renker, Elizabeth 10
Reveries of a Bachelor (Mitchell) 92
revolutions
  American 4, 12-13, 40, 71-4
  European Revolutions of 1848 28-9, 33-4, 85-6
  French 50-2, 110-11
  Haitian 85-6
  Latin American 89
Reynolds, Larry J. 41
Rights of Man (Paine) 112
Rogin, Michael Paul 34-5
Romanticism 47, 53-4, 57-8, 67, 70-1, 77, 104
Rome, Italy 50-2
Rousseau, Jean-Jacques 47

S

Said, Edward 53-4
Sanborn, Geoffrey 20
Sartre, Jean-Paul 44
Schopenhauer, Arthur 57
Sealts, Morton M., Jr. 117
"The Second Coming" (Yeats) 103-4
Sedgwick, Eve Kosofsky 113
self-formation 5-6, 31-3, 38, 41-3, 71
sex and sexuality 7-13, 21-3, 26-7, 39, 48, 67-8, 90, 92-4, 104-5, 108-9
Shakespeare, William 5, 10, 66-7
Shaw, Lemuel (father-in-law) 10, 21, 40-1, 52
Shelley, Mary 47, 61-2, 67, 91, 93
Silko, Leslie Marmon 78
Simms, William Gilmore 72
Sims, Thomas 52
skepticism 30, 56-7, 60, 63, 76-8, 100, 106-7, 113-14
The Sketch Book (Irving) 92
Smith, Adam 34-8
Spanos, William 53-4
Sparks, Jared 72
Spinoza, Baruch 58
spiritualism 75-6
Spivak, Gayatri 86-7
Stael, Madame de 67
"Statues of Rome" (1857) 108
Stella, Frank 44
Stowe, Harriet Beecher 9, 52, 67

Strauss, David Friedrich 104
Stuckey, Sterling 86–7
Swift, Jonathan 28–9
Sybil (Disraeli) 34

T

Tahiti, French Polynesia, 8, 24
taboo 22–3
Tai Pī people 8, 17
Tennyson, Alfred (Lord) 96–7
"That It Is Madness to Judge the True and the False" (Montaigne) 76
theodicy 62, 113–14
Thoreau, Henry David 40, 76, 81
Timoleon (1891) 95–6, 107–8
Timrod, Henry 97–8
Tocqueville, Alexis de 5
Tokarczuk, Olga 44
transcendentalism 67–8, 75–6
Tsang, Wu 44
Typee (1846) 8–10, 16–30, 44–5, 67, 74, 94, 111

U

Uncle Tom's Cabin (Stowe) 52
Updike, John 45–6

V

Vedder, Elihu 108

W

Warner, Susan 31–2
The Wealth of Nations (Smith) 34–7
Weaver, Raymond 14
Weber, Max 39, 49–50
Weeds and Wildings Chiefly (1891) 107–9
whaling industry 7–8, 49–50
"What to the Slave is the Fourth of July?" (Douglass) 72
White-Jacket (1850) 9–10, 30, 38–43, 45, 49–50, 65, 111–12
Whitman, Walt 17, 96–8
The Wide, Wide World (Warner) 31–2
Wilson, Harriet 34
Wordsworth, William 47, 96–7

Y

Yeats, William Butler 103–4
Young America movement 9–10, 68

ENGLISH LITERATURE
A Very Short Introduction
Jonathan Bate

Sweeping across two millennia and every literary genre, acclaimed scholar and biographer Jonathan Bate provides a dazzling introduction to English Literature. The focus is wide, shifting from the birth of the novel and the brilliance of English comedy to the deep Englishness of landscape poetry and the ethnic diversity of Britain's Nobel literature laureates. It goes on to provide a more in-depth analysis, with close readings from an extraordinary scene in King Lear to a war poem by Carol Ann Duffy, and a series of striking examples of how literary texts change as they are transmitted from writer to reader.

{No reviews}

www.oup.com/vsi

ROMANTICISM
A Very Short Introduction
Michael Ferber

What is Romanticism? In this *Very Short Introduction* Michael Ferber answers this by considering who the romantics were and looks at what they had in common – their ideas, beliefs, commitments, and tastes. He looks at the birth and growth of Romanticism throughout Europe and the Americas, and examines various types of Romantic literature, music, painting, religion, and philosophy. Focusing on topics, Ferber looks at the rising prestige of the poet; Romanticism as a religious trend; Romantic philosophy and science; Romantic responses to the French Revolution; and the condition of women. Using examples and quotations he presents a clear insight into this very diverse movement.

www.oup.com/vsi

Writing and Script
A Very Short Introduction
Andrew Robinson

Without writing, there would be no records, no history, no books, and no emails. Writing is an integral and essential part of our lives; but when did it start? Why do we all write differently and how did writing develop into what we use today? All of these questions are answered in this *Very Short Introduction*. Starting with the origins of writing five thousand years ago, with cuneiform and Egyptian hieroglyphs, Andrew Robinson explains how these early forms of writing developed into hundreds of scripts including the Roman alphabet and the Chinese characters.

'User-friendly survey.'

Steven Poole, The Guardian

www.oup.com/vsi

ENGLISH LANGUAGE
A Very Short Introduction
Simon Horobin

The English language is spoken by more than a billion people throughout the world. But where did English come from? And how has it evolved into the language used today?

In this *Very Short Introduction* Simon Horobin investigates how we have arrived at the English we know today, and celebrates the way new speakers and new uses mean that it continues to adapt. Engaging with contemporary concerns about correctness, Horobin considers whether such changes are improvements, or evidence of slipping standards. What is the future for the English language? Will Standard English continue to hold sway, or we are witnessing its replacement by newly emerging Englishes?

www.oup.com/vsi